HIDDEN
HERESY

HIDDEN HERESY

Is spiritualism invading Adventist churches today?

THOMAS MOSTERT

Pacific Press® Publishing Association
Nampa, Idaho
Oshawa, Ontario, Canada
www.pacificpress.com

Designed by Dennis Ferree
Cover photo: Liquid Library

Copyright © 2005 by
Pacific Press® Publishing Association
Printed in the United States of America
All rights reserved

Additional copies of this book are available by calling toll free
1-800-765-6955 or by visiting www.adventistbookcenter.com

ISBN: 0-8163-2115-9

05 06 07 08 09 · 5 4 3 2 1

CONTENTS

PREFACE

In early January 2005 I received a letter asking for my opinion on a document by an unknown author. It addressed some of the current trends in popular churches and suggested potential problems if Adventist churches took the same course. That letter and document started me on a study far more detailed than I had ever done on this subject. It also reinforced my concerns about some disturbing trends I had noticed in the church.

As I researched the positions of well-known churches and compared those findings with inspired counsel, my discoveries led to an ever growing set of notes. Later, when I shared my thinking with the conference presidents of the Pacific Union, they encouraged me to share the information more widely. What you have in your hands is a result of what I have discovered so far.

I hope what you find in these pages will bring a new awareness of the issues and a commitment to God's truth in your own life. This is the end time, and our loving Savior has shared with us—in His own words and through His prophets—everything we need to stay on course to the kingdom. He has given us guidance and warnings to help our church relate to the world around us.

Certain things I discovered as I studied were new to me, and they were obviously controversial. So I counseled with a number of people. I thank each one for taking the time to read the material and share their opinions and suggestions. Special thanks go to my friend Dr. Herb Douglass, who offered invaluable assistance and encouragement along the way. You should be aware that except where otherwise indicated, all bold type in this book represents emphasis that I have added. I have also included full quotations in most cases in order to better provide complete and correct context for the relevant portions cited.

You may or may not agree with my conclusions. But in any case, you will be more informed as to the veiled nature of spiritualism in the great controversy going on between Christ and Satan, and its present and future influence in the churches. I also hope your understanding and commitment to the Seventh-day Adventist mission will be expanded.

Thomas Mostert

CHAPTER

1

CAN YOU IDENTIFY MODERN SPIRITUALISM?

Spiritualism influencing the Adventist Church? "What a bizarre idea," you say. "How in the world could something so foreign to the very heart of Adventism possibly gain entry into this church? And what pastor or member would stand by and let it happen? That just isn't possible!"

But before you dismiss this idea as impossible, take the quiz below and see if you are really aware of the present façade of modern spiritualism. Its concepts have become accepted in the Christian church and now seem to be coming, unrecognized, through the back door of some Adventist churches.

> Spiritualism is now changing its form and, veiling some of its more objectionable features, is assuming a Christian guise. . . .
>
> Christ is as verily rejected as before; but Satan has so blinded the eyes of the people that the deception is not discerned (*The Great Controversy*, pp. 557, 558).

"Satan . . . comes to poor, deceived mortals, through modern spiritualism. . . . The world knows but little as yet of the corrupting influence of spiritualism. The curtain was lifted, and much of its dreadful work was revealed to me" (*Testimonies for the Church,* vol. 1, p. 343). And in the context of Satan's last great deception, Ellen White wrote, "The line of distinction between professed Christians and the ungodly is now hardly distinguishable. Church members love what the world loves and are ready to join with them, and Satan determines to unite them in one body and thus strengthen his cause by sweeping all into the ranks of spiritualism" (*The Great Controversy,* p. 588).

Can you identify veiled spiritualism?

Read the following statements carefully. Within these well-known non-Adventist theological teachings, see if you can spot those that prepare the way for spiritualism. *Circle the numbers that express spiritualistic concepts.* (**Note: You are looking for that which opens the door to spiritualism, not whether you agree with the theological viewpoint.**)

1. Through continuous spiritual consciousness, death no longer exists.
2. Sin is any act or thought that robs myself or another human being of his or her self-esteem.
3. To be born again means we must be changed from a negative to a positive self-image—from inferiority to self-esteem, from fear to love, from doubt to trust.
4. In the mind of Jesus, self-esteem is the ultimate human value. Christ came to teach that simple truth, and He came to live it.

5. Jesus Christ knew, in reality, there is no evil. Therefore evil is a false law man has made for himself.

6. All true believers are one with Christ and each other, regardless of denominational background.

7. "If I Accept Jesus Christ Is My Salvation Forever?" Definitely! Your salvation is through the most trustworthy being in the universe—Jesus Christ! You didn't do anything to earn your salvation, and you can't do anything to lose it. Your salvation is maintained by God's trustworthiness and love, not by what you do.

8. When you stand before God, He will not ask you about your religious background or doctrinal views. The only thing that will matter is: Did you accept Jesus?

9. If you want Jesus to come back sooner, focus on fulfilling your mission, not figuring out prophecies.

10. I invite you to bow your head and quietly whisper the prayer that will change your eternity: *"Jesus, I believe in you and receive you."* Go ahead. If you sincerely meant that prayer, congratulations. Welcome to the family of God.

If you circled all ten statements, you spotted veiled spiritualism. If you missed some, you will learn more in the following pages. (The source for each of the ten statements above is given at the end of this chapter.)

You will also recognize that most of these statements come from very popular and fast-growing churches. Since some Adventists are studying the church growth concepts of these churches, it is possible that while pursuing the worthy goal of growing the church, the door is opened to concepts that could have a corrupting influence.

The two great end-time errors

In the vast sweep of end-time events that will take place before Jesus comes, spiritualism and Sunday sacredness will play pivotal roles. They will contribute to the spiritual decline of the popular churches, even as these churches seem caught up in a grand revival. Ellen White describes the last deception in these words:

> **Through the two great errors, the immortality of the soul and Sunday sacredness, Satan will bring the people under his deceptions. While the former lays the foundation of spiritualism, the latter creates a bond of sympathy with Rome. The Protestants of the United States will be foremost in stretching their hands across the gulf to grasp the hand of spiritualism; they will reach over the abyss to clasp hands with the Roman power; and under the influence of this threefold union, this country will follow in the steps of Rome in trampling on the rights of conscience** (The Great Controversy, p. 588).

Sacredness of God's law

Satan began his rebellion in heaven with the clear goal of doing away with the law of God. That was one of the primary issues that caused him and a third of the angels to be cast out of heaven. It is still his primary goal, and through various means he is attempting to erase God's law from human consciousness. We must keep this clearly in mind as we move through this study, for it is the key issue that emerges again and again in the great controversy. "Satan grew bold in his rebellion, and expressed his contempt of the Creator's law. This Satan could not bear. He claimed that angels needed no law but should be left free to follow their own will, which would ever guide them right; that law was a restriction of their liberty; and that to abolish law was one great object of his" (*The Story of Redemption,* pp. 18, 19).

Because the children of men reject the plainest teachings of his word, and trample upon his law, God leaves them to choose that which they desire. They spurn the truth, and he permits them to believe a lie. They refuse to yield to the convictions of the Holy Spirit, and Satan, transforming himself into an angel of light, leads them captive at his will. If men were but conversant with the word of God, and obedient to its teachings, they could not be thus deceived; but they neglect the great detector of fraud, and the mind becomes confused and corrupted by the deceptive arts of men, and the secret power of the father of lies (*Signs of the Times,* May 18, 1882).

Marvelous beyond expression is the blindness of the people of this generation. **Thousands reject the word of God as unworthy of belief and with eager confidence receive the deceptions of Satan.** Skeptics and scoffers denounce the bigotry of those who contend for the faith of prophets and apostles, and they divert themselves by holding up to ridicule the solemn declarations of the Scriptures concerning Christ and the plan of salvation, and the retribution to be visited upon the rejecters of the truth. They affect great pity for minds so narrow, weak, and superstitious as to acknowledge the claims of God and obey the requirements of His law. They manifest as much assurance as if, indeed, they had made a covenant with death and an agreement with hell—as if they had erected an impassable, impenetrable barrier between themselves and the vengeance of God. **Nothing can arouse their fears. So fully have they yielded to the tempter, so closely are they united with him, and so thoroughly imbued with his spirit, that they have no power and no inclination to break away from his snare** (*The Great Controversy*, p. 561).

The substitution of the laws of men for the law of God, the exaltation, by merely human authority, of Sunday in place of the Bible Sabbath, is the last act in the drama. When this substitution becomes universal, God will reveal Himself (*Testimonies for the Church*, vol. 7, p. 141).

Veiled spiritualism
Spiritualism is the other great issue in end-time events. "**Satan determines to unite them [professed Christians and the ungodly] in one body and thus strengthen his cause by sweeping all into the ranks of spiritualism**" (*The Great Controversy*, p. 588). But it will take on a new look, dress in new clothes, and appear to be something it isn't.

Under this "Christian" guise, spiritualism successfully prepares people to accept the false teachings of evil spirits that directly contradict Scripture.

Those who oppose the teachings of spiritualism are assailing, not men alone, but Satan and his angels. They have entered upon a contest against principalities and powers and wicked spirits in high places. Satan will not yield one inch of ground except as he is driven back by the power of heavenly messengers. The people of God should be able to meet him, as did our Saviour, with the words: "It is written." **Satan can quote Scripture now as in the days of Christ, and he will pervert its teachings to sustain his delusions. Those who would stand in this time of peril must understand for themselves the testimony of the Scriptures.**

Many will be confronted by the **spirits of devils** personating beloved relatives or friends and **declaring the most dangerous heresies.** These visitants will appeal to our tenderest sympathies and will work miracles to sustain their pretensions. We must be prepared to withstand them with the Bible truth that the dead know not anything and that they who thus appear are the spirits of devils.

Just before us is "the hour of temptation, which shall come upon all the world, to try them that dwell upon the earth." Revelation 3:10. All whose faith is not firmly established upon the word of God will be deceived and overcome. Satan "works with all deceivableness of unrighteousness" to gain control of the children of men, and his deceptions will continually increase. But he can gain his object only as men voluntarily yield to his temptations. Those who are earnestly seeking a knowledge of the truth and are striving to purify their souls through obedience, thus doing what they can to prepare for the conflict, will find, in the God of truth, a sure defense. "Because thou hast kept the word of My patience, I also will keep thee" (verse 10), is the Saviour's promise. He would sooner send every angel out of heaven to protect His people than leave one soul that trusts in Him to be overcome by Satan (Ibid., pp. 559, 560).

Men of intelligence are **infatuated with Satanic sorcery** as verily today as in the days of Paul. **Thousands accept the opinion of the minister or obey the injunctions of the pope or priest, and neglect God's word and despise his truth.** God would have his people learn their duty for themselves. The Bible declares his will to men, and it is as much our privilege and our duty to learn that will as it is that of ministers and popes and priests to learn it. What they can read from God's word, we can all read (*Signs of the Times,* May 18, 1882).

It is true that spiritualism is now changing its form and, veiling some of its more objectionable features, it is assuming a Christian guise. . . .
Even in its present form, so far from being more worthy of toleration than formerly, it is really a more dangerous, because a more subtle, deception. While it formerly de-

nounced Christ and the Bible, it now *professes* to accept both. But the Bible is interpreted in a manner that is pleasing to the unrenewed heart, while its solemn and vital truths are made of no effect. Love is dwelt upon as the chief attribute of God, but it is degraded to a weak sentimentalism, making little distinction between good and evil. God's justice, His denunciations of sin, the requirements of His holy law, are all kept out of sight. The people are taught to regard the Decalogue as a dead letter. Pleasing, bewitching fables captivate the senses and lead men to reject the Bible as the foundation of their faith. Christ is as verily denied as before; but Satan has so blinded the eyes of the people that the deception is not discerned (*The Great Controversy*, pp. 557, 558).

Notice carefully how the quotation above details the subtle changes in the public face of spiritualism—changes all designed to create an atmosphere in which false teachers can tear down God's law. Notice that Ellen White points out five specific aspects to this veiled form of Satan's tool. All can now be seen in modern Christian churches:

1. **"The Bible is interpreted** in a manner that is pleasing to the unrenewed heart, while its solemn and **vital truths are made of no effect."**
2. **"Love is dwelt upon as the chief attribute of God,** but it is degraded to a weak sentimentalism, **making little distinction between good and evil."**
3. "God's justice, His denunciations of sin, **the requirements**

of His holy law, are all kept out of sight. The people are taught to regard the Decalogue as a dead letter."

4. **"Pleasing, bewitching fables captivate the senses** and lead men to reject the Bible as the foundation of their faith."

5. "Christ is . . . denied . . . ," but the **eyes of the people are blinded so that they don't see the deception.**

These concepts prepare the ground for the last great deception.

The line of distinction between professing Christians and the ungodly is now hardly distinguishable. Church members love what the world loves and are ready to join with them, **and Satan determines to unite them in one body and thus strengthen his cause by sweeping all into the ranks of spiritualism.** Papists, who boast of miracles as a certain mark of the true church, will be readily deceived by this wonder-working power; and Protestants, having cast away the shield of truth, will also be deluded. Papists, Protestants, and worldlings will alike accept the form of godliness without the power, and **they will see in this union a grand movement for the conversion of the world, and the ushering in of the long-expected millennium** (*The Great Controversy*, pp. 588, 589).

I was directed to this scripture as especially applying to modern spiritualism: Colossians 2:8: "Beware lest any man spoil you through philosophy and vain deceit, after the tradition of men, after the rudiments of the world, and not after Christ.". . .

"Vain deceit" fills the minds of poor mortals. They think there is such power in themselves to accomplish great works that they realize no necessity of a higher power. **Their principles and faith are "after the tradition of men, after the rudiments of the world, and not after Christ"** (*Mind, Character, and Personality,* vol. 2, p. 723).

Jesus has not taught them this philosophy. Nothing of the kind can be found in His teachings. He did not direct the minds of poor mortals to themselves, to a power which they possessed. He was ever directing their minds to God, the Creator of the universe, as the source of their strength and wisdom. Special warning is given in verse 18: "Let no man beguile you of your reward in a voluntary humility and worshiping of angels, intruding into those things which he hath not seen, vainly puffed up by his fleshly mind" (*Testimonies for the Church,* vol. 1, p. 297).

Inspiration describes other pieces of the end-time puzzle that help us understand more clearly how "the two great errors" are established. Jesus prophesied, "Many will turn away from me and betray and hate each other. And many false prophets will appear and will lead many people astray. Sin will be rampant everywhere, and the love of many will grow cold" (Matthew 24:10–12, NLT).

Paul said,

> And now, brothers and sisters, let us tell you about the coming again of our Lord Jesus Christ and how we will be gathered together to meet him. . . .
>
> For that day will not come until there is a great rebellion against God and the man of lawlessness is revealed— the one who brings destruction. He will exalt himself and defy every god there is and tear down every object of adoration and worship. He will position himself in the temple of God, claiming that he himself is God (2 Thessalonians 2:1–4, NLT).

The Bible declares that before the coming of the Lord there will exist a state of religious declension similar to that in the first centuries. "In the last days perilous times shall come. For men shall be *lovers of their own selves,* covetous, boasters, proud, blasphemers, disobedient to parents, unthankful, unholy, without natural affection, trucebreakers, false accusers, incontinent, fierce, *despisers of those that are good,* traitors, heady, high-minded, *lovers of pleasures more than lovers of God; having a form of godliness,* but denying the power thereof." 2 Timothy 3:1-5. "Now the Spirit speaketh expressly, that in the latter times some shall depart from the faith, giving heed to seducing spirits, and doctrines of devils." 1 Timothy 4:1. Satan will work "with all power and signs and lying wonders, and with all deceivableness of unrighteousness." And all that "received not the love of the truth, that they might be saved," will be left to accept "strong delusion, that they should believe a lie." 2 Thessalonians 2:9-11. When this state of ungodliness shall be reached, the same results will follow as in the first centuries.

The wide diversity of belief in the Protestant churches is regarded by many as decisive proof that no effort to secure a forced uniformity can ever be made. But there has been for years, in churches of the Protestant faith, a strong and growing sentiment in favor of a union based upon common points of doctrine. To secure such a union, the discussion of subjects upon which all were not agreed—however important they might be from a Bible standpoint—must necessarily be waived (*The Great Controversy*, p. 444).

By the pride of human wisdom, by contempt for the influence of the Holy Spirit, and by disrelish for the truths of God's word, many who profess to be Christians, and who feel competent to teach others, will be led to turn away from the requirements of God. Paul declared to Timothy, "The time will come when they will not endure sound doctrine; but after their own lusts shall they heap to themselves teachers, having itching ears; and they shall turn away their ears from the truth, and shall be turned unto fables." [2 Timothy 4:3-4.]

The apostle does not here refer to the openly irreligious, but to the professing Christians who make inclination their guide, and thus become enslaved by self. **Such are willing to listen to those doctrines only that do not rebuke their sins or condemn their pleasure-loving**

course. They are offended by the plain words of the faithful servants of Christ and choose teachers who praise and flatter them. And among professing ministers there are those who preach the opinions of men instead of the word of God. Unfaithful to their trust, they lead astray those who look to them for spiritual guidance (*Acts of the Apostles*, pp. 504, 505).

After describing in graphic detail how society will fall apart in the end time, Paul adds that the basic reason will be due to people acting "as if they are religious, but they will reject the power that could make them godly" (2 Timothy 3:5, NLT). Peter puts it this way: "I want to remind you that in the last days there will be scoffers who will laugh at the truth and do every evil thing they desire" (2 Peter 3:3, NLT).

Key to quiz references:

1. *Love, Medicine, and Miracles,* p. 220. Dr. Bernie Siegel, New Age/occult writer endorsed by Norman Vincent Peale.

2. *Self-Esteem: The New Reformation,* p. 14. Robert Schuller, Word Books, 1982.

3. Ibid., p. 68.

4. *Hour of Power* Web site. Robert Schuller. Spiritual Guidance section (basic beliefs) "The Greatest Day in the History of the World," February 4, 2005.

5. *The Game of Life,* p. 30. Florence Shinn, metaphysician, endorsed on the cover by Norman Vincent Peale. (Peale was the inspiration for Robert Schuller.)

6. Willow Creek Statement of Belief, *The Church.* From the Willow Creek Web site, February 4, 2005. Bill Hybels, founding pastor.

7. Saddleback Church Beliefs, Rick Warren, from the church Web site.

8. *The Purpose Driven Life,* p. 34. Rick Warren, Zondervan, 2002.

9. Ibid., p. 286.

10. Ibid., pp. 58, 59.

CHAPTER
2

UNDER THE RADAR

It is important to be aware of the forces working behind the scenes to bring down God's remnant church while there is time to do something about it. Recent developments in the Christian world may well be making inroads into the church under the radar.

In these pages we will explore in detail Satan's plans to take control of human minds through religious movements and churches. We will focus particularly on a new phenomenon known as the mega/gigachurch movement. It has arisen over the last twenty years with astonishing speed and is affecting Protestant churches in the United States in profound ways. While the problems we will discuss are not limited to the megachurches and gigachurches, we will focus on them only because they are so influential on Adventist churches. At the same time, we must realize God has many of His faithful followers in these churches, and many of their members and pastors are dedicated, committed Christians. Often, they are more committed to what they believe than are the members and leaders of the Adventist Church. "Notwithstanding the spiritual darkness and alienation from God that exist in the churches which constitute Babylon, the great body of Christ's true followers are still to be found in their communion. There are many of these who have never seen the special truths for this time" (*The Faith I Live By*, p. 285).

All through history God has led sincere people closer to him. He has worked through religious leaders such as Martin Luther and John Wesley to bring clearer understandings of truth. Even though most of these leaders failed to understand important areas of God's truth, He used them as instruments of reform. They were His voice in a sea of error. Today, growing churches seem to be experiencing these same divine blessings. Yet at some point sincere people and leaders will be taken captive by Satan to do his work in the name of Jesus—especially when they see end-time truths and the everlasting gospel in its purest form. Most Adventists think that time is still future, thus we have nothing to worry about in copying other churches' successful methods as long as we don't accept their theology. We will discover that this is not necessarily true.

It is no doubt impossible to fully know which religious leaders God is using and which may be unknowingly following a plan created by His enemy. The fruitage of most Christian leaders and churches today seems positive. Large numbers of lives are changed from a secular focus to a commitment to Jesus. People spend quality time studying Scripture and sharing spiritual insights with friends. People give generously of their time and money to advance the cause of God. All this seems to be the fruitage of a true relationship with Jesus.

If God is leading Sunday churches to save people for the kingdom, are they not doing a work that is beyond the reach of Adventists? Shouldn't we thank God for what is happening, use whatever good methods of theirs we can, and wait until the end-time events mature fully to worry about any dangers?

We could. But remember, Satan never uses a strategy that is too obvious. He is not only planning to use Sunday churches as part of his final great deception; he will also seek to sidetrack and neutralize the work of God's remnant church.

In this study we will identify certain beliefs and practices in Christian churches that seem to hold prophetic significance. But please understand that I am not passing judgment on other Christians. God will lead sincere people closer to Him using all sorts of methods and churches, as the Holy Spirit leads them, step by step, into the fullness of the everlasting gospel. But at the same time, Satan also plans to use earnest, dedicated people for his purposes.

Adventists need to be aware of the potential danger for the church and our own lives in the events now unfolding around us. Therefore, it is important to know the main players, what they believe, and how they may be used in the great controversy between Christ and Satan.

Understanding the gigachurch movement

Many U.S. congregations have grown so large that the term "megachurch" no longer seems adequate. So some observers have created a new category: the "gigachurch."

"Where 'megachurch' refers to congregations with an average of 2,000 or more worshipers every weekend, 'gigachurch' refers to those with 10,000 or more," said Texas-based church consultant Bill Easum, adding that the rising number of large congregations reflects a major shift in worship patterns. "Today, fully 3 million church attendees go to a megachurch vs. 897,000 only ten years ago," Easum writes in the current issue of *Outreach*, an evangelical magazine published in Vista, California.

Thirty-five of the congregations on the list of megachurches did not even exist a decade ago. **The landscape of the Christian church is changing faster than at any other point in American history.**

"The flagship church of this change, in terms of size and speed of growth, is Lakewood Church in Houston," said John N. Vaughn, a leading analyst of the megachurch phenomenon. Lakewood posts an average attendance of 25,060 per weekend—nearly twice its attendance five years ago and 8,000 more than Willow Creek Community Church near Chicago, which two decades ago set the standard for megachurch development.

With its move next spring to a 16,000-seat sanctuary, the $73 million remodeled Compaq Center—former home to the Houston Rockets—Lakewood is on track to become the first U.S. church to surpass 30,000 in attendance," Vaughn said (Bill Broadway, *Washington Post* staff writer, Saturday, May 15, 2004).

There are 820 mega/gigachurches in the United States. Note where the largest numbers are located: California (125); Texas (111); Florida (53); Georgia (44); Maryland (30); Illinois (30); Michigan (30); Minnesota (26); Tennessee (26); Washington (25); Indiana (23); New York (23); Oklahoma (23); Ohio (23); North Carolina (19); Alabama (18); Colorado (17);

Arizona (16); Pennsylvania (16); Missouri (14); Louisiana (13); Virginia (13); Washington, D.C. (12); Oregon (11); Kansas (11); Kentucky (11). Other states have less than ten. The following states do not have any megachurches on record: Maine, Montana, New Hampshire, Rhode Island, South Dakota, Utah, Vermont, West Virginia, and Wyoming. (Hartford Institute for Religion Research, Hartford Seminary, 77 Sherman Street, Hartford, Connecticut. From the Web site <hirr.hartsem.edu>.)

Some of the largest gigachurches

David Yonggi Cho: Yoido Full Gospel Church in Seoul is located in South Korea, and has 750,000 members. Paul Yonggi Cho, pastor of the world's largest church, claims to have received his call to preach from Jesus Christ Himself, who supposedly appeared to him dressed like a fireman. (Dwight J. Wilson, "Cho, Paul Yonggi," *Dictionary of Pentecostal and Charismatic Movements*, p. 161.) Cho has packaged his faith formulas under the label of "fourth dimensional power." (According to Cho, the material world makes up the first three dimensions, which are under the control of the fourth dimension—the spirit.) He is well aware of his link to occultism, arguing that if Buddhists and Yoga practitioners can accomplish their objectives through fourth dimensional powers, then Christians should be able to accomplish much more by using the same means. (Paul Yonggi Cho, *The Fourth Dimension* [South Plainfield, N.J.: Bridge Publishing, 1979], vol. 1, pp. 37, 41.)   In case one is tempted to confuse the size of Cho's following with the truth of his teachings, let me point out that the Buddhist version of "name it and claim it" (Nichiren Shoshu Buddhism) has an even larger following than does Cho. (See John Weldon, "Nichiren Shoshu Buddhism: Mystical Materialism for the Masses," *Christian Research Journal*, Fall 1992, pp. 8–13.) Cho recently made the news by changing his name from Paul to David. As Cho tells the story, God showed him that Paul Cho had to die and David Cho was to be resurrected in his place. According to Cho, God Himself came up with his new name. (Paul Yonggi Cho, interviewed by C. Peter Wagner, "Yonggi Cho Changes His Name," *Charisma & Christian Life*, November 1992, p. 80.)

Joel Osteen: The largest church in the United States is Lakewood Church in Houston, Texas. Pastor Joel Osteen preaches to some 30,000 people each week. Known throughout the world as a model for racial harmony and diversity, Lakewood Church has become a congregation of nearly equal numbers of Caucasian, Hispanic, and African-American members. Each week, Lakewood produces television programming that is broadcast to millions of people worldwide. In addition, it has audiotape and videotape duplication and a publication facility that sends teaching materials to more than one hundred countries.

The late John Osteen was a pastor, evangelist, author, and teacher for sixty years until he died in 1999. Ordained as a Southern Baptist minister, he received the baptism in the Holy Ghost in 1958, an experience that revolutionized his ministry outreach for Jesus Christ. John Osteen held a bachelor's degree from John Brown University, a master's degree from Northern Baptist Seminary, a doctor of letters from Indiana Christian University, and a doctor of divinity from Oral Roberts University. His son Joel now leads the ministry.

T. D. Jakes: In 1979, Bishop Jakes founded Greater Emmanuel Temple of Faith, a small storefront church in Montgomery, West Virginia, that originated with only ten members. In only five years since relocating the church from West Virginia to Dallas, Texas, The Potter's House grew from fifty families to more than 28,000 members.

Mac Brunson: First Baptist Church, Dallas, Texas, has 25,000 members. Founded in 1868, it has had only eight pastors since its beginning, and only two pastors, George Truett and W. A. Criswell, for the period 1897 through 1995, when Dr. Criswell was named pastor emeritus after serving for fifty years.

Chuck Smith: Calvary Chapel is located on eleven acres in Costa Mesa, California. In the past three decades the church has grown from only 25 to 25,000 members. It has as many as 30,000 people in its congregation each week. There are almost seven hundred affiliated Calvary Chapels throughout America and the rest of the world.

Bishop Eddie Long: Bishop Long pastors 25,000 members at New Birth Missionary Baptist Church, Decatur, Georgia.

Earl Paulk: Founded in the heart of inner city Atlanta, Georgia, the Cathedral at Chapel Hill has a staff of 25 full-time pastors working with 25,000 members.

Creflo Dollar: World Changers Ministries is a global ministry organization anchored by the 23,500-member World Changers Church International in College Park, Georgia.

Rick Warren: Saddleback Church in Lake Forest, California, has 22,000 members with a mailing list of over 80,000 names.

Rick Warren is one of the leaders many are following. Pastors are paying to download his sermons from his pastors.com Web site. His book *The Purpose Driven Church* has sold more than a million copies. In 2003 he followed it with the best-selling nonfiction hardcover book of all time, *The Purpose Driven Life*. It has now sold more than twenty-two million copies. Since the Ashley Smith encounter in Atlanta, Georgia, in which Ashley used this book to calm a criminal, Rick Warren has appeared on all the major talk shows and news programs. Hundreds of Adventist churches are studying this book—or have been. This one pastor is a force to be reckoned with!

V. Hilliard: New Light Christian Center Church in Houston, Texas, has 20,000 members.

Paul S. Morton, Sr.: Saint Stephen Full Gospel Baptist Church in New Orleans, Louisiana, has 20,000 members.

Keith A. Butler: Pastor Butler is the founder and senior pastor of Word of Faith International Christian Center, a congregation of more than nineteen thousand members in Southfield, Michigan.

Betty Peebles: Jericho City of Praise in Landover, Maryland, in the Washington, D.C., area has 19,000 members.

Edwin Young: Second Baptist Church in Houston, Texas is one church in three locations with a total of 18,000 members.

Paula White: Paula White co-pastors the 18,000-member Without Walls International Church, based in Tampa, Florida, with her husband, Randy.

Fred Price: Crenshaw Christian Center in Inglewood, California, a suburb of Los Angeles, has 18,000 members.

Ed Young: Fellowship Church, on three campuses, is located in the heart of the Dallas-Fort Worth area. The church's main campus sits on 141 acres just north of DFW airport. The church has 16,000 members.

Kerry Shook: In eleven years Fellowship of the Woodlands (Houston, Texas, area) has grown to 12,000 in average attendance each Sunday.

Bill Hybels: At Willow Creek Community Church in suburban Chicago, 17,000 attend each week. The church has 10,000 members.

John Hagee: Cornerstone Church in San Antonio, Texas, has more than seventeen thousand active members.

Greg Laurie: Harvest Christian Fellowship in Riverside, California, has 15,000 members.

Adrian Rogers: Bellevue Baptist Church in Cordova, Tennessee (near Memphis), has 14,000 members.

Bill Winston: Living Word Christian Center in Chicago has over twelve thousand members.

Rod Parsley: World Harvest Church, located in Columbus, Ohio, has 12,000 members.

Billy Joe Daugherty: Pastor Daugherty leads Victory Christian Center, an 11,000-member church in Tulsa, Oklahoma.

Robert Schuller: The Crystal Cathedral in Garden Grove, California, has over ten thousand members.

Bishop Clarence McClendon: Bishop McClendon's Church of the Harvest International, in historic Hollywood Palladium auditorium, is strategically located in the heart of Hollywood, California. It has 10,000 members; 12,000 people in weekly attendance.

Jim Cymbala: Brooklyn Tabernacle in New York City has 10,000 members.

John Wimber: John Wimber founded the first Vineyard Church in Anaheim, California, in 1982. Today there are 850 members. **The Association of Vineyard Churches is one of the fastest growing church-planting movements in the world.**

From the beginning, Vineyard pastors and leaders have sought to hold in tension the biblical doctrines of the Christian faith with an ardent pursuit of the present day work of the Spirit of God. Maintaining that balance is never easy in the midst of rapid growth and renewal.

John Wimber was a founding leader of the Vineyard. His influence profoundly shaped the theology and practice of Vineyard churches from their earliest days until his death in November 1997. When John was conscripted by God he was, in the words of *Christianity Today,* a "beer-guzzling, drug-abusing pop musician, who was converted at the age of 29 while chain-smoking his way through a Quaker-led Bible study" (*Christianity Today,* editorial, Feb. 9, 1998).

In John's first decade as a Christian he led hundreds of people to Christ. By 1970 he was leading 11 Bible studies that involved more than 500 people. Under God's grace, John became so fruitful as an evangelical pastor he was asked to lead the Charles E. Fuller Institute of Evangelism and Church Growth. He also later became an adjunct instructor at Fuller Theological Seminary where his classes set attendance records. In 1977, John reentered pastoral ministry to plant Calvary Chapel of Yorba.

Throughout this time, John's conservative evangelical paradigm for understanding the ministry of the church began to grow. George Eldon Ladd's theological writings on the kingdom of God convinced John intellectually that all the biblical gifts of the Holy Spirit should be active in the church. Encounters with Fuller missiologists Donald McGavaran and C. Peter Wagner and seasoned missionaries and international students **gave him credible evidence for combining evangelism with healing and prophecy.** As he became more convinced of God's desire to be active in the world through all the biblical gifts of the Spirit, John began to teach and train his church to imitate Jesus' full-orbed kingdom ministry. He began to "do the stuff" of the Bible that he had formerly only read about.

As John and his congregation sought God in intimate worship they experienced empowerment by the Holy Spirit, significant renewal in the gifts and conversion growth. It became clear that the church's emphasis on the experience of the Holy Spirit was not shared by some leaders in the Calvary Chapel movement. In 1982, John's church left Calvary Chapel and joined a small group of Vineyard churches. Vineyard was a name chosen by Kenn Gulliksen, a prolific church planter affiliated with Calvary Chapel, for a church he planted in Los Angeles in 1974. Pastors and leaders from the handful of Vineyard churches began looking to John for direction. And the Vineyard movement was born.

Twenty years later, there are more than 850 Vineyard churches worldwide, an international church planting movement, a publishing house and a music production company. Vineyard worship songs have helped thousands of churches experience intimacy with God. Many churches have been equipped to continue Jesus' ministry of proclaiming the kingdom, healing the sick, casting out demons and training disciples. (From The Vineyard Community of Churches Web site <www.vineyardusa. org/ about/history.aspx>.)

The signs and wonders movement: The term "third wave" was first coined by C. Peter Wagner in 1983:

I see historically that we're now in the third wave. The first wave of the moving of the Holy Spirit began at the beginning of the century with the Pentecostal movement. The second wave was the charismatic movement which began in the fifties in the major denominations. Both of those waves continue today.

I see the third wave of the eighties as an opening of the straight-line evangelicals and other Christians to the supernatural work of the Holy Spirit that the Pentecostals and charismatics have experienced, but without becoming either charismatic or Pentecostal. I think we are in a new wave of something that now has lasted almost through our whole century (Peter Wagner, "The Third Wave?" *Pastoral Renewal,* July–August 1983, pp. 1–5).

This movement is also called the signs and wonders movement and the vineyard movement. It has been a rapidly growing movement, drawing adherents from both charismatic and non-charismatic churches. The movement stresses "power evangelism" whereby the gospel is explained and demonstrated by way of supernatural signs and wonders.

There are three key leaders of this movement: (1) John Wimber, probably the central figure of the movement. He founded the vineyard church movement upon coming out of Chuck Smith's Calvary Chapel movement, and he taught with C. Peter Wagner at Fuller Seminary. The course was titled "Signs, Wonders, and Church Growth." (2) C. Peter Wagner, professor at Fuller Seminary School of World Missions, where he co-taught with John Wimber. (3) Paul Cain, an influential "modern day prophet," a disciple of William Branham, whom Cain called "the greatest faith healer of our time" and the "greatest prophet of all time."

In the signs and wonders movement, tongues speaking can be found, but the gift of tongues is not stressed as much as it is in the Pentecostal and charismatic movements. The signs and wonders movement (vineyard movement) does stress the gift of prophecy (insisting on the importance of modern-day prophets) and the gift of healing. (Adapted from the Appendix of a paper, "The Charismatic Movement: 35 Doctrinal Issues," by Pastor George Zeller.)

Seventh-day Adventists: At the same time as other churches are growing, it is a painful fact that many of the Seventh-day Adventist churches in North America are not growing. Those that are tend to be institutional churches or those attracting immigrant populations. As a result, pastors and members are thinking that maybe they, too, should follow what seems to be working so well for others. You will notice the large number of gigachurches and megachurches disbursed around the country. Their presence creates a reality that has our pastors and members thinking and copying.

Adventists attend all types of church growth seminars and buy church growth books by the dozens, yet they are frustrated over the small numbers present in their churches on Sabbath morning. They look at Willow Creek, Saddleback, and other superchurches, and ask, "Why do we have to grow so slowly? Why are we hearing no winning formulas from our own church? We emphasize church planting, but none of our new plants have grown into superchurches." The contrast has many wondering and others making changes.

But before we adopt the ways and thinking of others, we need to clearly understand how Satan has woven his own thinking into the popular churches of the world. We will see how his thinking is already affecting the remnant church.

CHAPTER
3

MEGA/GIGACHURCHES AND THE LAST GREAT DECEPTION

As I have studied in detail various megachurches and giga-churches, it seems to me that the characteristics of the last great deception to be created by Satan at the end of time are woven into the fabric of most of these churches right now. While no one can know precisely where we are in the fulfillment of end-time prophecy or what other events and manifestations are yet to come, it seems to me that we already see in the gigachurches and megachurches elements that are tracking along the prophetic path that will allow people to be deceived by Satan.

God has given His church a detailed picture of the final events and has warned us to stay away from this path. Yet, we already see some pastors and members using methods and theological concepts to grow Adventist churches without seeming to realize where they lead or the mastermind behind them.

A closer look at Saddleback, Willow Creek, and Crystal Cathedral

In the light of what we know is coming, let's take a closer look at the nature and thinking of the three gigachurches most studied by Adventist ministers in the United States: Saddleback,

Willow Creek, and Crystal Cathedral. Although many mega-churches and gigachurches are out there, Adventists tend to turn away from those that are Pentecostal in nature. It is clear to most Adventists that faith healing and speaking in tongues is not the model for us to follow. The African-American megachurches and gigachurches have some features that we sometimes copy, but no one church seems to have become a model. In light of the runaway success of the two "purpose driven" books, Saddleback is now the church model that is most copied.

Saddleback—"purpose driven"

The February 7, 2005, issue of *Time* magazine had a cover article on "The 25 Most Influential Evangelicals in America." **Number one on the list is Southern California pastor Rick Warren, founding pastor of the 22,000-member Saddleback Community Church in Tustin, California.** When six hundred senior pastors were asked to name the individuals they thought had the greatest influence on church affairs in the country, Warren's name came in second only to Billy Graham's. Many believe Warren is the successor to Graham for the role of "America's minister."

Warren's book *The Purpose Driven Life* has sold more than twenty-two million copies in the last two years and is the best-selling nonfiction hardback book in U.S. history. His book *The Purpose Driven Church* has sold over one million copies since 1995. It has been translated into more than twenty-five languages and was voted one of the one hundred Christian books that changed the twentieth century. More than 350,000 church leaders from 120 countries have been trained in

Saddleback's purpose-driven paradigm. Warren has mentored more than a hundred thousand congregations worldwide.

Hundreds of Adventist churches have joined the thousands of churches around the world in the forty-day spiritual journey through the book *The Purpose Driven Life*. It claims to be a blueprint for Christian living in the twenty-first century. Using more than twelve hundred scriptural quotes and references, it challenges the conventional definitions of worship, fellowship, discipleship, ministry, and evangelism. The abundance of Scripture would seem to make its message safe.

Rick Warren is a major force in the Christian world. More than any other single person, he is influencing the thinking and program of Adventist churches. We must take a careful look at what he is saying and ask where it will lead us. Is his philosophy in harmony with the Adventist mission—and if not, in what ways?

Already, we are seeing the fruitage of Warren's influence in Adventist churches. Pastors in several conferences have announced that they are no longer going to preach controversial doctrines from the pulpit. They indicate their plan is to become "seeker sensitive" on Sabbath morning. The format will be entertaining because that is what nonmembers want. The music will be contemporary. Each has indicated to members who object, "If you don't like the new direction, transfer to another church." It is not coincidental that these same suggestions can be found on Warren's Web site, pastors.com, where a pastor details how he changed an established church to follow the Warren model.

Let's be clear that both *The Purpose Driven Church* and *The Purpose Driven Life* are outstanding books. Most of what they teach would be hard to argue with. In fact, they are two of the most practical books you will ever read. If Adventist churches used some of the principles described in *The Purpose Driven Church,* there would be growth beyond anything we have ever seen. Rick Warren understands what makes a church work. His concepts of living the truth as he sees it, organizational principles, and the importance of small groups are right on target.

For example, in themselves, these aspects of *The Purpose Driven Church* could be considered as part of God's plan:

• Highly organized well-planned worships

Angels work harmoniously. Perfect order characterizes all their movements. The more closely we imitate the harmony and order of the angelic host, the more successful will be the efforts of these heavenly agents in our behalf. **If we see no necessity for harmonious action, and are disorderly, undisciplined, and disorganized in our course of action, angels, who are thoroughly organized and move in perfect order, cannot work for us successfully.** They turn away in grief, for they are not authorized to bless confusion, distraction, and disorganization (*Christian Experience and Teachings,* p. 199).

• Small groups grow people and evangelize

The formation of small companies as a basis of Christian effort has been presented to me by One who cannot err (*Christian Service,* p. 72).

• Multiple ministries to reach the community

Our Saviour went from house to house, healing the sick, comforting the mourners, soothing the afflicted, speaking peace to the disconsolate. He took the little children in His arms and blessed them, and spoke words of hope and comfort to the weary mothers. With unfailing tenderness and gentleness, **He met every form of human woe and affliction.** Not for Himself, but for others did He labor. He was the servant of all. It was His meat and drink to bring hope and strength to all with whom He came in contact (*Gospel Workers,* p. 188).

Jesus worked to relieve every case of suffering that He saw. He had little money to give, but He often denied Himself of food in order to relieve those who appeared more needy than He. His brothers felt that His influence went far to counteract theirs. He possessed a tact which none of them had, or desired to have. When they spoke harshly to poor, degraded beings, Jesus sought out these very ones, and spoke to them words of encouragement. To those who were in need He would give a cup of cold water, and would quietly place His own meal in their hands. As He relieved their sufferings, the truths He taught were associated with His acts of mercy, and were thus riveted in the memory (*The Desire of Ages*, p. 87).

The positive side of Warren's "purpose driven" concepts is well described in the following article:

HIDDEN HERESY

The Purpose Driven Church Model: Can It Work for You? ©

by John W. Ellas[1]

Bill Hybels and the Willow Creek Community Church are frequently credited with starting a renewal movement in worship among U.S. congregations. Likewise, I believe Rick Warren and the Saddleback Community Church will receive credit for beginning another type of renewal—getting churches back to discovering and working toward fulfilling their God-given purposes.

One of the most prevalent problems among churches of Christ is the condition of institutionalism. Most newly planted churches begin with an urgent sense of purpose (what God wants accomplished as revealed in his Word) and vision (how to accomplish the different aspects of the purpose in the local context). This type of start typically results in healthy growth. After a decade or two, institutionalism often sets in when members lose a clear and urgent awareness of the church's purpose. The same routine ministry activities are repeated over and over as if they were the purpose rather than a means to accomplish the end (the God-given purpose.) The loss of a clear and urgent purpose produces non-growing churches doing the same things the same way with little regard for the end results, and often reluctant to make any changes.

---

[1] John W. Ellas is editor of *Church Growth* magazine since 1994. He has written *Church Growth Through Groups: Clear Choices for Churches* and *Measuring Church Growth*. This article was published in *Church Growth* magazine, January–March, 2000, pp. 2–4.

No one has done a better job of clarifying, in simple terms, the purpose of the church than Rick Warren in *The Purpose Driven Church* (Zondervan, 1995). More importantly, he has shown that leaders can design a ministry strategy that is driven not by traditions but by God's multifaceted purpose for the church revealed in scripture and that God is still giving the increase through effective planting and watering.

It's important to recognize that a church's subculture is experienced not in what they say is important, but rather in what they do. For example, most churches will say they have a commitment to local evangelism, but in fact it is only an *aspirational value.* If they are actually reaching the unchurched and the church's data supports the claim, then it is a *core value.* The combination of real core values expressed in church life produces its subculture (also called a church's personality).

It would require numerous pages to explore fully each of Warren's core values revealed in *The Purpose Driven Church.* Several are outlined here to help leaders implement the transferable principles.

PDC Core Values

1. *Ministry design is driven by a clear Biblical purpose* (p. 95ff). Warren is correct when he observes that every church is driven by something. It might be traditions, finances, programs, or facilities. In most cases, congregations are not aware of their own core values. At Saddleback, the five purposes of the church are written,

communicated, and incorporated in every aspect of church life.

Can your leader and members articulate the purpose of the church? How urgent is your congregation about fulfilling its purpose?

2. *Evangelistic outreach to the unchurched is a dominant core value for Saddleback.* From the very start every decision made in developing the PDC model places a priority on mission (reaching the lost) rather than maintenance (serving the members). Here are a few examples: the church's location (pp. 33, 34), discourages transfers (p. 39), did not start the church with a core of Christians (p. 138), ministries target the needs of the unchurched (p. 222), visitor-friendly assemblies (p. 211), and worship designed with the seeker in mind (p. 249).

How many of these values reside in your congregation? And how many are they willing to adopt?

3. *A high demand disciple-making process is a core value in order to turn new converts into committed disciples.* This value is made tangible by strategies behind the "five circles of commitment" and the "life development process" (pp. 127–134). For new members to become a part of the leadership core, they are required to attend specific training classes and sign ministry agreements.

What level of accountability are your members willing to accept?

4. *Proactive leadership is exercised through every dimension of church life.* Warren accurately understands the pulpit minister's role and the impact of communication (pp. 111–

118). A church will move in the direction of its most dominant thoughts. Another way to understand this is whatever is regularly communicated in the pulpit by ministers and elders will set the foundation for congregational core values and its direction. Leaders should be regularly communicating and praying with the church about the purpose and goals of the congregation.

The second aspect of proactive leadership is regular meetings with volunteer leaders for training and motivation (p. 143). Warren considers the monthly leaders meeting a high priority.

How effective are your leaders exercising proactive leadership? Are they willing to learn and apply leadership skills? Are members willing to follow?

5. *Ministry is measured and evaluated, and adjustments are made.* Warren insists that their purpose and vision statements are put in measurable terms (pp. 93, 101, 107). Every ministry is evaluated based on the church's purposes (p. 93). They are even willing to evaluate their assemblies and get visitor feedback (pp. 211, 275). This is possible only if churches meticulously keep accurate records and track statistics (pp. 151, 152). But most important, they are willing to abandon nonproductive ministries (pp. 90, 142).

How well is your church tracking data? And how willing are your members to accept changes?

These are only five of nearly a dozen core values revealed in *The Purpose Driven Church*. None of them is incidental. Rather they are integral for the effective implementation of the PDC model, and many are essential for any approach to growth.

This article is not written to discourage churches from using the PDC model. But I'll leave you with Rick Warren's own wisdom and advice: "Saddleback's story of growth is a sovereign act of God that cannot be replicated. However we should extract the lessons and principles that are transferable" (p. 66).

So why not just follow the principles Rick Warren used to grow his church? After all, you can't argue with his success: from 0 to 10,000 members in 15 years. And that was with no church building! They met in rented auditoriums. After they bought 120 acres and built a campus, they went on to grow to 22,000 members over the next 9 years. There are 175 full-time staff members. Along the way they started 25 new churches, sent out dozens of missionaries, and kept 75 ministries going to meet the needs of the community and members. And this is no independent church. They are part of the Southern Baptist Convention.

While much Rick Warren has done can be used by Adventists, we must also be aware of the pitfalls of his program and its limited gospel principles.

Willow Creek—pioneering mass appeal
Unlike Saddleback, Willow Creek Community Church in suburban Chicago is an independent church not affiliated with any denomination. The founding pastor, Bill Hybels, is another on *Time* magazine's list of the twenty-five most influential evangelical pastors in America. He is a graduate of Trinity College in

Hartford, Connecticut. He, too, appeals to an upscale, youthful crowd, with an informal yet rousing contemporary service and program. He also appeals to Adventist pastors who have flocked by the hundreds to his training programs over the last thirty years. In fact, Hybels trains more than a hundred thousand pastors each year. He leads a network of 10,500 churches built after his model.

On Saturday night and Sunday morning, Willow Creek's focus on "seekers" attracts over seventeen thousand worshipers. The membership is over six thousand.

Hybels often works with Rick Warren and Robert Schuller in conducting training programs.

Crystal Cathedral—possibility living

Fifty years ago, in 1955, Robert Schuller came to Garden Grove, California, to found a Reformed Church in America congregation. With his wife as organist and five hundred dollars in assets, he rented the Orange drive-in theater and conducted Sunday services from the roof of the snack bar. Using the concepts of "possibility thinking," the congregation grew and finally built the internationally acclaimed Crystal Cathedral. Its weekly services, called *The Hour of Power*, are now televised to more stations around the world than any other church service.

In light of the issues we have already addressed, this concept from one of Schuller's sermons is significant: "The Holy Bible gives the emotional power of optimism! Turning people into optimists is a big, big thing in contemporary psychological and psychiatric thinking. Some of my dear friends, Martin E. Seligman to name one, are specialists in it."

In an interview with Wendy Schman, a producer of *Beliefnet*, Martin Seligman, recent president of the American Psychological Association, admitted he does not believe in God and also said, "Part of my concern is the enormous number of people who, like myself, have no religious beliefs, and yet want to lead a meaningful life." Yet Seligman is a man whom Schuller calls "my dear friend" and whose concepts come through in Schuller's preaching.

How does Schuller view evangelism? In "Sharing Your Faith," a sermon he preached on September 30, 2001, Schuller said: "For 2000 years, religion has always seen itself with one mission: To tell everybody what we believe, to tell them that what we believe is the truth, and to try to convert other people to realize they aren't getting the whole truth and they've got to convert and become like we are. Protestants have done that against Catholics. Catholics against Protestants. Christians against Muslims and Christians against Jews. That kind of religion should drop to the dust the way the World Trade Towers fell in the terrorist attacks of 9-11-2001. It cannot continue."

Schuller believes the second coming of Jesus took place at Pentecost, and thus he does not believe in the eschatological return at the end of the world. Here is some additional Schuller theology taken from his book *Self Esteem: The New Reformation*:

- Yes, what we need in the world-wide Christian church today is nothing less than a new reformation. Where the sixteenth century Reformation **returned our focus to sacred Scriptures** as the only infallible rule for faith and practice, the new reformation will **return our focus to the sacred right of every person to self-esteem** (p. 38).

- Sin is any act or thought that robs myself or another human being of his or her self-esteem (p. 14).
- **A person is in hell when he has lost his self-esteem** (p. 15).
- **Self-esteem, then, or "pride in being a human being," is the single greatest need** facing the human race today (p. 19).
- It is precisely at this point that **classical theology has erred in its insistence that theology be "God-centered," not "man-centered"** (p. 64).
- Classical theology defines sin as "rebellion against God." The answer is not incorrect as much as it is **shallow and insulting to the human being** (p. 65).
- To be **born again** means that we must be **changed from a negative to a positive self-image, from inferiority to self-esteem, from fear to love, from doubt to truth** (p. 68).
- **God's master plan is designed around the deepest needs of human beings—self-dignity, self-respect, self-worth, self-esteem** (pp. 71, 72).
- Reformation theology failed to make clear that the **core of sin is a lack of self-esteem. . . .** At the same time, any creed, any Biblical interpretation, and any systematic theology that **assaults or offends the self-esteem of persons is heretically failing to be truly Christian** (pp. 135, 136).

- **The great error of classical theology is not starting with the value of the person,** but treating them as "unworthy sinners." The result has been the glorification of human shame in Christian theology (p. 180).

It is important to note that Rick Warren spent time with Schuller right out of seminary and before he started Saddleback. He credits Schuller with the concept of finding out what people want and shaping a program to meet those needs. Warren has a recommendation from Schuller in the front of his book *The Purpose Driven Church*.

Schuller is the author of more than thirty books, including five that have appeared on the *New York Times* bestseller list. Each year, Schuller trains hundreds of ministers on how to grow a church, sometimes joining Rick Warren and Bill Hybels.

CHAPTER
4

DANGERS IN MIXING TRUTH AND ERROR

It is time to take a close look at the Saddleback philosophy. Church leaders must have a clear understanding of the issues involved in the "purpose driven" concept. Where can we support it? Where must we be careful? At the same time we will compare Rick Warren's positions with the thinking of Joel Osteen, Bill Hybels, and Robert Schuller because they have many similarities. Mixed in with all the good are some subtle dangers we have been told Satan will use in the last days.

The following material is all taken from direct sources, including books and Web sites. In general, it is not so much what is taught but, rather, what is left out that makes these concepts so dangerous. The law of God is mentioned only a few times, and when it is, the reference is in general terms, not to any one commandment or specific lifestyle actions. This is important in light of Satan's original opposition to God's law and his strategy of a veiled spiritualism that keeps God's law in the background while professing to believe in it. All this allows evil spirits access to sincere hearts.

Notice the church doctrines shown below to which one must agree in order to become a member of the Saddleback church. Observe how no mention is made of the law of God or obedience.

What We Believe

1. God is bigger and better and closer than we can imagine.
2. The Bible is God's perfect guidebook for living.
3. Jesus is God showing himself to us.
4. Through His Holy Spirit, God lives in and through us now.
5. Nothing in creation "just happened." God made it all.
6. Grace is the only way to have a relationship with God.
7. Faith is the only way to grow in our relationship with God.
8. God has allowed evil to provide us with a choice, God can bring good even out of evil events, and God promises victory over evil to those who choose him.
9. Heaven and hell are real places.
10. Death is a beginning, not the end.
11. The church is to serve people like Jesus served people.
12. Jesus is coming again.

Willow Creek statement of faith

Now read the Willow Creek Statement of Faith. While it includes the word *obedience,* it doesn't define what that means.

THE WILLOW CREEK STATEMENT OF FAITH summarizes our beliefs as a church. Our theology is not innovative—anyone familiar with historic Christian doctrine will find that these statements fall in the center of evangelical theology ("evangelical" means theology derived from the evangel, or the Gospel; in other words, it's biblical theology rather than speculative theology or theology rooted in tradition). We try not to be dogmatic about matters on which Bible-based believers have held divergent views. We want our core beliefs to be centered in Christ and His message as found in and supported by the clearest passages of Scripture. More obscure doctrine or teachings with less support are left to individuals to sort out on their own—we take no official position in these areas.

1. **THE SOLE BASIS OF OUR BELIEF IS THE BIBLE,** composed of the 66 books of the Old and New Testament.

2. **WE BELIEVE THAT THERE IS ONE TRUE, HOLY GOD,** eternally existing in three persons—Father, Son and Holy Spirit—each of whom possesses equally all the attributes of deity and the characteristics of personality.

3. **THE CENTRAL PURPOSE OF GOD'S REVELATION** in Scripture is to call all people into fellowship with Himself.

4. **JESUS CHRIST IS THE ETERNAL SECOND PERSON OF THE TRINITY** who was united forever with a true human nature by a miraculous conception and virgin birth.

5. **THE ESSENTIAL ACCOMPANIMENT** of a genuine saving relationship with Jesus Christ is a life of

holiness and obedience, attained by believers as they submit to the Holy Spirit, the third Person of the Trinity.

6. **DEATH SEALS THE ETERNAL DESTINY** of each person. For all mankind, there will be a resurrection of the body into the spiritual world and a judgment that will determine the fate of each individual.

7. **THE COROLLARY OF UNION** with Jesus Christ is that all believers become members of His body, the Church. There is one true Church universal, comprised of all those who acknowledge Jesus Christ as Savior and Lord.

8. **SCRIPTURE IS THE FINAL AUTHORITY** in all matters of faith and practice. This church recognizes that it cannot bind the conscience of individual members in areas where Scripture is silent. Rather, each believer is to be led in those areas by the Lord, to whom he or she alone is ultimately responsible.

   COMMENTS: We believe what we have said in this Statement of Faith is not teaching of our own design, but an accurate reflection of the Bible's main themes, true for all people at all times in every place. This final statement simply asks that everyone in our fellowship agree that, even if they have differing opinions, there be no divisiveness.

Crystal Cathedral/Hour of Power statement of faith

Notice how the statement of faith from the Crystal Cathedral likewise omits obedience and the law of God:

Crystal Cathedral/Hour of Power Statement of Faith

Our Beliefs:

About God

1. God is the Creator and the Ruler of the universe.
2. He is the Father of Jesus Christ.
3. He is our Father and will provide for all the needs of our bodies and souls.
4. He is present everywhere.

About Jesus Christ

1. Jesus Christ is the only begotten Son of God.
2. He gave His life as the perfect sacrifice for the sins of the world.
3. He arose from the dead and is alive forevermore.
4. He is King of kings and will be finally victorious over all evil.

About the Holy Spirit

1. The Holy Spirit is co-equal with the Father and the Son, three persons in the triune God.
2. He is "the other Comforter" who dwells in the hearts of men, convincing them of the truth of Christ's teachings, and helping them do right.

About Man

1. Man is by nature sinful and cannot make himself good.
2. He can only be made righteous by accepting God's

forgiveness for sin through Jesus' sacrifice on the cross.

3. He will be given a new life because of his relation to Jesus Christ.

4. He is designed for everlasting life.

About the Bible

1. The Bible is the inspired Word of God.

2. It is our only guide to show us what we should believe and how we should live.

3. It is for everyone to read so that all may hear God speak to their hearts and minds.

About the Church

1. The church is made up of people of every race who believe in Jesus Christ.

2. Jesus Christ is the Head of the church, and the members are His Body.

3. Children of church members are called "children of the covenant." Their baptism is a sign and seal of this covenant relationship and of their membership in the Christian church.

4. The task of the church is to make Jesus Christ known throughout the whole world.

About the Sacraments

1. We have two sacraments, instituted by Christ in the new covenant, or testament. They are baptism and the holy supper, **or communion.**

Notice, again, how the statement of faith from the Crystal Cathedral omits any emphasis on obedience and God's law.

Lakewood Church statement of faith

The statement of faith from Joel Osteen's Lakewood Church also omits obedience and the law of God:

WE BELIEVE. . .

- The Bible is the inspired and only infallible and authoritative Word of God. Salvation has been provided and is available for people through Jesus Christ. Through His sacrifice on the cross, we can die to our sinful nature and be born again to a new life of purity and power.
- Water baptism is a symbol of the cleansing power of the blood of Christ and a testimony to our faith in the Lord Jesus Christ.
- The baptism in the Holy Spirit, according to Acts 2:4, is given to believers who ask for it, provides power to live a sanctified and holy life and to be effective in service to God.
- As children of God, we are overcomers and conquerors and have authority over the devil and his works.

Services at Lakewood Church

We minister to the Lord in worship. Each service begins with joyous songs of praise, prayer and worship.

- We minister to people. We pray for the sick, comfort the hurting and sorrowful, encourage the weak and weary,

and reach out in love to those who need a friend.
- We minister the Word of God. The proclamation of the Gospel comes after individuals have opened their hearts to God and turned from themselves to others. Only then are they truly ready to hear and benefit fully from the Word of the Lord.

Why do we speak in tongues and have interpretation of tongues?

"For if I pray in a tongue, my spirit prays, but my mind is unfruitful. So what shall I do? I will pray with my spirit, but I will also pray with my mind; I will sing with my spirit, but I will also sing with my mind" (1 Corinthians 14:14, 15).

"Therefore, my brothers, be eager to prophesy, and do not forbid speaking in tongues" (1 Corinthians 14:39).

"If anyone speaks in a tongue, two—or at the most three—should speak, one at a time, and someone must interpret" (1 Corinthians 14:27).

What it means to be "saved"

It means that we believe and trust in Jesus and the blood He shed.

1. By the blood of Jesus we have forgiveness of sins.
2. By the blood of Jesus we have peace with God.
3. By Jesus' sacrifice we no longer are afraid of God, we are children of God.
4. By the blood of Christ our consciences are cleansed.

5. By the blood of Jesus we gain bold access to the throne of God for prayer and worship.
6. We can receive forgiveness when we do sin after we are saved.
7. By the blood of Jesus we are able to conquer the accuser of the brethren, Satan.

To be "saved" means that we are "justified"

"To be justified" means we are made "right" with God! When God sees us, He doesn't see our sins, He sees the blood of Jesus.

"For all have sinned and fall short of the glory of God, and are justified freely by His grace through the redemption that came by Christ Jesus. God presented Him as a propitiation (a sacrifice that would turn aside the wrath of God by taking away sin) through faith in His blood" (Romans 3:23-25).

"He [Jesus] was delivered over to death for our sins and was raised to life for our justification" (Romans 4:25).

God now sees us "just as if we had never sinned!"

We now stand clothed in righteousness before God because we accepted the sacrifice of Jesus.

The "purpose driven" concepts and Adventism

We will focus now on a few specific teachings in Rick Warren's two best-selling books—*The Purpose Driven Church* and *The Purpose Driven Life*—with which Adventists do not agree. The following are areas in which these two books conflict with the Bible and with Adventism:

1. PDL: **"Wherever you are reading this, I invite you to bow your head and quietly whisper the prayer that will change your eternity:** *"Jesus, I believe in you and receive you."* **Go ahead. If you sincerely meant that prayer, congratulations. Welcome to the family of God"** (pp. 58, 59).

Jesus went into Galilee, proclaiming the good news of God. "The time has come," he said. "The kingdom of God is near. Repent and believe the good news!" (Mark 1:14, 15, NIV).

There is a spurious experience prevailing every-where. Many are continually saying, "All that we have to do is to believe in Christ." They claim that faith is all we need. In its fullest sense, this is true; but they do not take it in the fullest sense. To believe in Jesus is to take Him as our redeemer and our pattern. If we abide in Him and he abides in us, we are partakers of His divine nature, and are doers of his word. The love of Jesus in the heart will lead to obedience to all His commandments. But the love that goes no farther than the lips, is a delusion; it will not save any soul. Many reject the truths of the Bible, while they profess great love for Jesus; **but the apostle John declares, "He that saith, I know him, and keepeth not His commandments, is a liar, and the truth is not in Him." While Jesus has done all in the way of merit, we ourselves have something to do in the way of complying with the conditions. "If ye love me," said our Saviour, "keep my commandments"**

DANGERS IN MIXING TRUTH AND ERROR

(Ellen G.White, *Historical Sketches of the Foreign Missions of the Seventh-day Adventists* [1886], pp. 188, 189).

But the doctrine is now largely taught that the gospel of Christ has made the law of God of no effect; that by "believing" we are released from the necessity of being doers of the word. But this is the doctrine of the Nicolaitans, which Christ so unsparingly condemned. [Revelation 2:2-6 quoted] . . .

Those who are teaching this doctrine today have much to say in regard to faith and the righteousness of Christ; but they pervert the truth, and make it serve the cause of error. They declare that we have only to believe on Jesus Christ, and that faith is all-sufficient; that the righteousness of Christ is to be the sinner's credentials; that this imputed righteousness fulfills the law for us, and that we are under no obligation to obey the law of God. This class claim that Christ came to save sinners, and that He has saved them. "I am saved," they will repeat over and over again. But are they saved while transgressing the law of Jehovah?—No; for the garments of Christ's righteousness are not a cloak for iniquity. Such teaching is a gross deception, and Christ becomes to these persons a stumbling-block as He did to the Jews,—to the Jews because they would not receive Him as their personal Saviour; to these professed believers in Christ, because they separate Christ and the law, and regard faith as a substitute for obedience. They separate the Father and the Son, the Saviour and the world. Virtually they teach, both by precept and example, that Christ, by His death, saves men in their transgressions (*Signs of the Times,* February 25, 1897).

2. PDC: "Choosing a neutral name was an evangelism strategy, not a theological compromise" (p. 199).

The name Seventh-day Adventist carries the true features of our faith in front, and will convict the inquiring mind. Like an arrow from the Lord's quiver, it will wound the transgressors of God's law, and will lead to repentance toward God and faith in our Lord Jesus Christ" (*Testimonies for the Church,* vol. 1, p. 224).

3. PDL: "There is no 'one-size-fits-all' approach to worship and friendship with God. One thing is certain: You don't bring glory to God by trying to be someone he never intended you to be. God wants you to be yourself" (p. 103).

The reason many in this age of the world make no greater advancement in the divine life is because they interpret the will of God to be just what they will to do. While following their own desires, they flatter themselves that they are conforming to God's will. These have no conflicts with self (*The Acts of the Apostles,* p. 565).

4. PDC: "At Saddleback, we expect of our members only what the Bible clearly expects of all believers. We summarize these expectations in our membership covenant" (p. 320).

Nowhere in the membership covenant do you find anything said about the law of God as a standard or of the importance of obedience, except in the general term, "living a godly life." But "a godly life" is never defined. Even the section on obedience in *The Purpose Driven Life* gives no specifics except for "such simple acts as telling the truth, being kind, and encouraging others" (p. 96). How can you teach people to be "blameless and pure" if it is not defined? "Do everything without complaining or arguing, so that you may become blameless and pure, children of God without fault in a crooked and depraved generation, in which you shine like stars in the universe" (Philippians 2:14, 15 NIV).

The Saddleback Membership Covenant

Having received Christ as my Lord and Savior and been baptized, and being in agreement with Saddleback's statements, strategy, and structure, I now feel led by the Holy Spirit to unite with the Saddleback church family. In doing so, I commit myself to God and to the other members to do the following:

1. I will protect the unity of my church
. . . by acting in love toward other members.
. . . by refusing to gossip.
. . . by following the leaders.

"So let us concentrate on the things which make for harmony, and on the growth of our fellowship together" (Rom. 14:19, Phillips).

"Have a sincere love for other believers, love one another earnestly with all your heart" (1 Peter 1:22, TEV).

"Do not let any unwholesome talk come out of your mouths, but only what is helpful for building others up according to their needs" (Eph. 4:29).

"Obey your leaders and submit to their authority. They keep watch over you as men who must give an account. Obey them so that their work will be a joy, not a burden, for that would be no advantage to you" (Heb. 13:17).

2. I will share the responsibility of my church
. . . by praying for its growth.
. . . by inviting the unchurched to attend.
. . . by warmly welcoming those who visit.

"We always thank God for you and pray for you constantly" (1 Thess. l: l, 2, LB).

"The Master said to the servant, 'Go out to the roads and country lanes, and urge the people there to come so my house will be full' " (Luke 14:23, NCV).

"So; warmly welcome each other into the church, just as Christ has warmly welcomed you; then God will be glorified" (Rom. 15:7, LB).

3. I will serve the ministry of my church
. . . by discovering my gifts and talents.
. . . by being equipped to serve by my pastors.
. . . by developing a servant's heart.

"Serve one another with the particular gifts God has given each of you" (1 Peter 4:10, Phillips).

"[God] gave . . . some to be pastors and teachers, to prepare God's people for works of service, so that the body of Christ may be built up" (Eph. 4:11, 12).

"Each of you should look not only to your own interests, but also to the interests of others. Your attitude should be the same as that of Christ Jesus: Who . . . [took on] the very nature of a servant" (Phil. 2:4, 5–7).

4. I will support the testimony of my church
. . . by attending faithfully.
. . . by living a godly life.
. . . by giving regularly.

"Let us not give up meeting together . . . but let us encourage one another" (Heb. 10:25).

"Whatever happens, make sure that your everyday life is worthy of the gospel of Christ" (Phil. 1:27, Phillips).

"Each one of you, on the first day of each week, should set aside a specific sum of money in proportion to what you have earned and use it for the offering" (1 Cor. 16:2, LB).

"A tenth of [all your] produce . . . is the Lord's, and is holy" (Lev. 27:30, NCV).

Satan is presenting worldly attractions. The churches are teaching for doctrine the commandments of men. Ministers are crying, "There is no law," failing to see

that if there is no law, there is no transgression. It is time for us to show that we have a message from the Lord, a message of no human invention. Workers who will present the truth in its simplicity are greatly needed. The last message of warning is to be given to the world. As God's people bring the truths of His message into the daily life, practical godliness, purity, and holiness will be seen (*Manuscript Releases,* vol. 5, p. 54).

The gospel of good news was not to be interpreted as allowing men to live in continued rebellion against God by transgressing His just and holy law. Why cannot those who claim to understand the Scriptures, see that God's requirement under grace is just the same He made in Eden—perfect obedience to His law. **In the judgment, God will ask those who profess to be Christians, Why did you claim to believe in My Son, and continue to transgress My law? Who required this at your hands— to trample upon My rules of righteousness?** "Behold, to obey is better than sacrifice, and to hearken than the fat of rams." The gospel of the New Testament is not the Old Testament standard lowered to meet the sinner and save him in his sins. **God requires of all His subjects obedience, entire obedience to all His commandments. He demands now as ever perfect righteousness as the only title to heaven. Christ is our hope and our refuge. His righteousness is imputed only to the obedient. Let us accept it through faith, that the Father shall find in us no sin. But those who have trampled on the holy law**

will have no right to claim that righteousness. O that we might view the immensity of the plan of salvation as obedient children to all God's requirements, believing that we have peace with God through Jesus Christ, our atoning sacrifice (RH Sept. 21, 1886)! (6BC, pp. 1072, 1073).

5. PDL: "If you want Jesus to come back sooner, focus on fulfilling your mission, not figuring out prophecy" (p. 286).

As we near the close of this world's history, the prophecies relating to the last days especially demand our study. The last book of the New Testament scriptures is full of truth that we need to understand. Satan has blinded the minds of many, so that they have been glad of any excuse for not making the Revelation their study. But Christ through His servant John has here declared what shall be in the last days, and He says, "Blessed is he that readeth, and they that hear the words of this prophecy, and keep those things which are written therein." Rev. 1:3 (*Christ's Object Lessons*, p. 133).

6. "If I Accept Jesus Christ Is My Salvation Forever? Definitely! Your salvation is through the most trustworthy being in the universe—Jesus Christ! You didn't do anything to earn your salvation, and you can't do anything to lose it. Your salvation is maintained by God's trustworthiness and love not by what you do" (Rick Warren, "Saddleback Church Beliefs," from the church Web site).

In the professedly Christian world many turn away from the plain teachings of the Bible and build up a creed from human speculations and pleasing fables, and they point to their tower as a way to climb up to heaven. Men hang with admiration upon the lips of eloquence while it teaches that the transgressor shall not die, that salvation may be secured without obedience to the law of God. If the professed followers of Christ would accept God's standard, it would bring them into unity; but so long as human wisdom is exalted above His Holy Word, there will be divisions and dissension. The existing confusion of conflicting creeds and sects is fitly represented by the term "Babylon," which prophecy (Revelation 14:8; 18:2) applies to the world-loving churches of the last days (*Patriarchs and Prophets,* p. 124).

7. PDC: "Saddleback is unapologetically a contemporary music church. We've often been referred to in the press as 'the flock that likes to rock' " (p. 285).

The Holy Spirit never reveals itself in . . . a bedlam of noise. This is an invention of Satan to cover up his ingenious methods for making of none effect the pure, sincere, elevating, ennobling, sanctifying truth for this time. Better never have the worship of God blended with music than to use musical instruments to do the work which last January was represented to me would be brought into our camp meetings. The truth for this time needs nothing of this kind in its work of converting souls. A bedlam of noise shocks the senses and perverts that which if conducted aright might be a blessing. The powers of satanic agencies blend with the din and noise, to have a carnival, and this is termed the Holy Spirit's working (*Selected Messages,* bk. 2, p. 36).

Popular revivals are too often carried by appeals to the imagination, by exciting the emotions, by gratifying the love for what is new and startling. Converts thus gained have little desire to listen to Bible truth, little interest in the testimony of prophets and apostles. **Unless a religious service has something of a sensational character, it has no attractions for them.** A message which appeals to unimpassioned reason awakens no response. The plain warnings of God's Word, relating directly to their eternal interests, are unheeded (*The Great Controversy,* p. 463).

8. PDC: "Never criticize what God is blessing" (p. 62).

In many of the revivals which have occurred during the last half century, the same influences have been at work, to a greater or less degree, **that will be manifest in the more extensive movements of the future.** There is an emotional excitement, a mingling of the true with the false, that is well adapted to mislead. Yet none need be deceived. In the light of God's Word it is not difficult to determine the nature of these movements. Wherever men neglect the testimony of the Bible, turning away from those plain, soul-testing truths which require self-denial and renunciation of the world, there we may be sure that God's blessing is not bestowed. And by the rule which Christ Himself has given, "Ye shall know them by their fruits" (Matt. 7:16), it is evident that these movements are not the work of the Spirit of God (Ibid., pp. 464, 465).

Before the final visitation of God's judgments upon the earth there will be among the people of the Lord such a revival of primitive godliness as has not been witnessed since apostolic times. The Spirit and power of God will be poured out upon His children. At that time many will separate themselves from those churches in which the love of this world has supplanted love for God and His word. Many, both of ministers and people, will gladly accept those great truths which God has caused to be proclaimed at this time to prepare a people for the Lord's second coming. **The enemy of souls desires to hinder this work; and before the time for such a movement shall come, he will endeavor to prevent it by introducing a counterfeit.** In those churches which he can bring under his deceptive power **he will make it appear that God's special blessing is poured out; there will be manifest what is thought to be great religious interest. Multitudes will exult that God is working marvelously for them, when the work is that of another spirit.** Under a religious guise, Satan will seek to extend his influence over the Christian world (Ibid., p. 464).

CHAPTER
5

WHAT'S WRONG WITH "SEEKER FOCUSED"?

Another issue to understand in the philosophy of some growing Sunday churches is the concept of being "seeker focused." We are not alone in our concern over this emphasis.

John MacArthur, a Southern California pastor with a church—Grace Community Church—close to Warren's, points out what can happen when a church is "seeker focused" as is Saddleback. MacArthur can be heard on the *Grace to You* radio program, which broadcasts daily around the world on nearly two thousand stations in English and Spanish. Grace Community Church's two morning worship services fill the 3,500-seat auditorium to capacity. He is also president of The Master's College and Seminary as well as a best-selling author.

In his book *Ashamed of the Gospel: When the Church Becomes Like the World,* **MacArthur warns against preaching and teaching a candy-coated gospel that neither offends nor convicts anyone.** He challenges the church to return to the roots of the Great Commission. Notice what he says in this July 24, 2003, article from his Web site—Grace to You.

Recently, the 11th edition of the Merriam-Webster's

Collegiate Dictionary was published. The reprint included 10,000 new words—words that will bring us all up to date. Words like "phat" (excellent), "dead presidents" (paper currency), and "McJob" (low paying, dead-end job) are among the entries that will finally help us communicate with our teenagers.

How did those words make it into the updated dictionary? There is one criterion: usage. A word qualifies for the new edition based on how widespread its usage has become. While I can't imagine how "phat," "McJob," and "dead presidents" will find a place in America's pulpits (e.g., The love of dead presidents is the root of all kinds of evil?), there is one phrase borrowed from the computer industry that has spread into mainstream usage in the church—its impact has been monumental.

"User-friendly" was first used to describe software and hardware that is easy for the novice to operate. Applied to the church, it describes churches that offer a decidedly benign and non-challenging ministry model. In practice, it has become an excuse for importing worldly amusements into the church in an attempt to attract non-Christian "seekers" or the "unchurched" by appealing to their fleshly interests. The obvious fallout of this preoccupation with the unbelievers is a corresponding neglect of true believers and their spiritual needs.

If you want to know how user-friendly a church has become, the emphasis, or de-emphasis, on biblical preaching is the yardstick. A church that buys into the new paradigm sidelines provocative and convicting sermons for music, skits, or videos—less confrontational mediums for conveying the message. Even when there is a sermon, it is frequently psychological and motivational rather than biblical. Above all, entertainment value and user-friendliness are paramount.

I once read through a stack of newspaper and magazine articles that highlight a common thread in the user-friendly phenomenon. These observations from newspaper clippings describe the preaching in user-friendly churches:

- "There is no fire and brimstone here . . . just practical, witty messages."
- "Services at [the church featured in the article] have an informal feeling. You won't hear people threatened with hell or referred to as sinners. The goal is to make them feel welcome, not drive them away."
- "As with all clergymen [this pastor's] answer is God— but he slips Him in at the end, and even then doesn't get heavy. No ranting, no raving. No fire, no brimstone. He doesn't even use the H-word. Call it Light Gospel. It has the same salvation as the Old Time Religion, but with a third less guilt."
- "The sermons are relevant, upbeat, and best of all, short. You won't hear a lot of preaching about sin and damnation, and hell fire. Preaching here doesn't sound like preaching. It is sophisticated, urbane, and friendly talk. It breaks all the stereotypes."
- "[The pastor] is preaching a very upbeat message. . . . It's a salvationist message, but the idea is not so much being

saved from the fires of hell. Rather, it's being saved from meaninglessness and aimlessness in this life. It's more of a soft-sell."

So the new rules may be summed like this: Be clever, informal, positive, brief, friendly, and never, never use the H-word.

The pastors and leaders in the church-growth movement certainly wouldn't portray their own ministries in that way. In fact, they would probably laud their success in drawing people into the church without compromising the message. But they fail to understand that by decentralizing the Scripture and avoiding hard truths, they are compromising. "For whoever is ashamed of me and my words, of him will the Son of man be ashamed when he comes in his glory, and the glory of the Father and of the holy angels" (Luke 9:26, RSV). If the design is to make the seeker comfortable, isn't that rather incompatible with the Bible's own emphasis on sin, judgment, hell, and several other important topics?

The gospel message is a confrontational message. When you remove the confrontation—or soften, downplay, or bring it in through the back door—you have compromised the message. The modern pulpit is weak, not for a lack of witty messages, but because men fear to speak the hard truths of God's Word powerfully and with conviction.

The church is certainly not suffering from an overabundance of forthright preachers; rather, it seems glutted with men pleasers (cf. Gal. 1:10). But, as it was in the early church, when men are faithful to preach God's Word with boldness, God will give the increase. "And they were continually devoting themselves to the apostles' teaching. . . . then fear came upon every soul. . . . and the Lord added to the church daily those who were being saved" (Acts 2:42, 43, 47).

When a sinner wanders into the church and sits through skits, mimes, interpretive dances, and the like, and yet never hears a clear, convicting message about his dangerous and tenuous spiritual situation—that he is a depraved sinner headed for an eternal fire because he is a daily offense to a holy God—how can that be called successful? You could achieve the same level of success by sending a cancer patient to receive treatment from a group of children playing doctor. A sinner must understand the imminent danger he is in if he is ever to look to the Savior.

C. H. Spurgeon, facing a similar mindset in his day, once said: *"I fear there are some who preach with the view of amusing men, and as long as people can be gathered in crowds, and their ears can be tickled, and they can retire pleased with what they have heard, the orator is content, and folds his hands, and goes back self-satisfied. But Paul did not lay himself out to please the public and collect the crowd. If he did not save them he felt that it was of no avail to interest them. Unless the truth had pierced their hearts, affected their lives, and made new men of them, Paul would have gone home crying, 'Who hath believed our report, and to whom is the arm of the Lord revealed?'. . .*

"Now observe, brethren, if I, or you, or any of us, or all of us, shall have spent our lives merely in amusing men, or educating men, or moralizing men, when we shall come to give our account at the last great day we shall be in a very sorry condition, and we shall have but a very sorry record to render; for of what avail will it be to a man to be educated when he comes to be damned? Of what service will it be to him to have been amused when the trumpet sounds, and heaven and earth are shaking, and the pit opens wide her jaws of fire and swallows up the soul unsaved? Of what avail even to have moralized a man if still he is on the left hand of the judge, and if still, 'Depart, ye cursed,' shall be his portion?" ["Soul Saving Our One Business," *The Metropolitan Tabernacle Pulpit,* vol. 25, (London: Passmore and Alabaster, 1879), 674–676.]

That is precisely my concern about today's pragmatic church-growth trend. The strategy focuses on attracting and keeping the unchurched. For what? To entertain them? To get them to attend church meetings regularly? Merely "churching" the unchurched accomplishes nothing of eternal value. That is where their strategy seems to end.

What's worse is when seeker-focused churches baptize the masses with their watered-down gospel, assuring them that positive decisions, feelings, or affirmations about Christ equal genuine conversion. There are now multitudes who are not authentic Christians identifying with the church. The church is literally invaded with the world's values, the world's interests, and the world's citizens. It isn't an invasion prompted by overt hostility; people are simply responding to a survey that came in the mail. Ironically, Satan isn't sowing the tares; church leaders are.

As you set your strategy for church ministry, you dare not overlook the primary means of church growth: the straightforward, Christ-centered proclamation of the unadulterated Word of God. If you trade the Word for amusements or gimmicks, you will not only find that you have no effective means to reach people with the truth of Christ, but you will find yourself working against the Lord Himself.[1]

George Barna echoes a similar concern when he writes:

To the average American, truth is relative to one's values and circumstances. Only one out of every four adults—and even fewer teenagers—believe that there is such a thing as absolute moral truth. The Bible is relegated to nothing more than a book of riveting stories and helpful suggestions. Human reason and emotion become the paramount determinants of all that is desirable and appropriate. This condition may be the single most intense threat to the health of the United States and its people.

Consider the social implications. Without an objective standard of right and wrong, laws and regulations become recommendations rather than mandates. Rights

---

[1] Adapted from *Ashamed of the Gospel: When the Church Becomes Like the World,* © 1993 by John MacArthur. All rights reserved.

are nothing more than sets of competing preferences. There can be no such thing as deception, only differing vantage points. Personal claims to authority and to the exercise of related power are susceptible to unsubstantiated challenges. Without accepted guideline pillars to anchor reality, those who succeed are the ones who argue loudest, most convincingly, and most diligently.

This cultural perspective hardens the hearts and deafens the ears of those who embrace it. **Without absolute moral truth, there can be no right and wrong. Without right and wrong, there is no such thing as sin. Without sin, there can be no such thing as judgment and no such thing as condemnation. If there is no condemnation, there is no need for a Savior. This progression renders the death and resurrection of Jesus Christ historically unique—and eternally meaningless** (George Barna, *The Second Coming of the Church*, p. 62).

Smith and Dutton's discovery

Notice how the declining emphasis on moral absolutes is revealing itself in our society. *Christianity Today*, April 2005, reported on an extensive survey of youth, ages thirteen to seventeen, titled *National Study of Youth and Religion,* done in 2004 by Smith and Denton. It had this to say about the study:

What Smith and Denton found out when they sat down to talk with teens one-on-one . . . should rock the world of every church in the country: In spite of their generally positive attitude toward religion, almost no teenagers, from any religious background, can articulate the most basic beliefs of their faith. This interview excerpt, with a fifteen-year old who attends two church services every Sunday . . . illustrates how vaguely most teenagers answered a question about their personal beliefs: **"Are there any beliefs that are important to you?"** "I think that you should just, if you're gonna do something wrong then you should always ask for forgiveness and he's gonna forgive you no matter what, cause he gave up his only Son . . . for you."

So what is the religion that teens hold in such high regard? Smith and Denton sum it up as "moralistic therapeutic deism"—the belief that religion is about doing good and being happy, watched over by a distant and benign Creator whose purpose is largely to help us feel better about ourselves.

And where do teenagers learn this faith . . . ? The evidence is overwhelming: There is no generation gap, and they love church. So they learned it from their parents—they learned it from their churches. Even their conservative Protestant churches.

The temptation to adopt "gospel lite"

It is tempting to lower our standards as a way to attract more people. You can do it directly or accomplish the same effect by not preaching or teaching those things that make people uncomfortable. Yet, that is the very purpose of the church. Paul wrote to the young pastor Titus, "We are instructed to turn from godless living and sinful pleasures. We should live in this evil world with self-control, right conduct, and devotion to God. . . . He [Jesus] gave his life to free us from every kind of sin, to cleanse us, and to make us his very own people, totally committed to doing what is right. **You must teach these things and encourage your people to do them, correcting them when necessary**" (Titus 2:12–15, NLT).

The fruitage of churches that fail to point out sin and call people to repentance is members who call themselves Christians, yet go their own way. Here is what John H. Armstrong, writing in *Viewpoint,* has to say on this:

In his important book, *Willow Creek Seeker Services* (Baker, 1996), religious sociologist G. A. Pritchard underscores, with data and careful study, the history of what is really behind the decision to invite a person like Bill Clinton to speak (at Willow Creek). Pritchard demonstrates that historically **Willow Creek has never stressed the transcendent moral law as a means to show people the holiness of God and the utter depravity of sinful humanity** (261–264). Pritchard tells how a church-wide survey was conducted which revealed the sad fact that large percentages of the Willow Creek congregation were admittedly guilty of regularly breaking God's Law. In the six months prior to the survey 33 percent of those in the congregation had lied, 18 percent had stolen, 12.5 percent had committed adultery, and 27 percent of the men had viewed pornography.

What did Hybels, the respected pastoral leader, do in light of these tragic moral indicators about the lives of thousands of his flock? He responded by telling the congregation that this behavior was not acceptable but then complimented them by adding: "Put your chest out a little bit—we are acknowledging our unrighteousness and we are exposing it to grace and truth. And we are banding together learning how we can have it forgiven and learning how the Holy Spirit can help us walk a little differently next week and next month and next year" (264).

Pritchard observes, **"The audience had not repented. They had not confessed their sin.** They had merely noted on a survey form that they had committed adultery, viewed pornography, and so on" (264).

This revelation was followed the very next week by a report on the singles (singles make up 25 percent of the total congregation). Hybels noted that large percentages of these single adults had "admitted having an illicit sexual relationship in the last six months" (264). But again, given the opportunity to preach on God's law and the cultivation of distinctive Christian ethics, emphasizing God's transcendent holiness, Hybels mixed distinctively therapeutic language with theology and said: "We are a love-starved people, with broken parts that need the kind of repair that only He can give long-term. We need to bring our brokenness out into the light of his grace and truth" (264). No warnings based upon passages like 2 Corinthians 13:5 or 2 Peter 1:10 were even mentioned. Pritchard rightly concluded, "This is a subtle process of emphasizing the truth of God's loving compassion and willingness to forgive, which has distorted the truth about God's holiness" (265).

Here's the real point. What is going on in the above examples is a complete and radical reshaping of historic doctrinal Christianity. Few evangelicals recognize it and fewer still are willing to say anything about it if they do recognize it. Princeton sociologist Robert Wuthnow suggests that in modern America "God has been modeled to satisfy people's needs" (Pritchard, 260). (*Viewpoint,* September–October 2000, vol. 4, no. 5).

CHAPTER

6

SPIRITUALISM IN MODERN DRESS

Here is veiled spiritualism at work: "The Bible is interpreted in a manner that is pleasing to the unrenewed heart, while its solemn and vital truths are made of no effect. Love is dwelt upon as the chief attribute of God, but it is degraded to a weak sentimentalism making little distinction between good and evil. God's justice, His denunciations of sin, the requirements of His holy law, are all kept out of sight" (*The Great Controversy*, p. 558). **"Many religious teachers assert that Christ by His death abolished the law, and men are henceforth free from its requirements. There are some who represent it as a grievous yoke, and in contrast to the bondage of the law they present the liberty to be enjoyed under the gospel"** (Ibid., p. 466).

Adventists, in contrast, are called not only to tell people about the love of God but to issue a call to live for Him as well.

If you lower the standard in order to secure popularity and an increase of numbers, and then make this increase a cause of rejoicing, you show great blindness. If numbers were an evidence of success, Satan might claim the pre-eminence; for, in this world, his followers are largely in the majority. . . . It is the virtue, intelligence, and piety of the people composing our churches, not their numbers, that should be a source of joy and thankfulness (*Counsels to Teachers,* p. 94).

We need divine wisdom and skill that we may improve every opportunity that the providence of God shall prepare for the presentation of truth. **While Satan will make masterly efforts to suppress truth, we must stand firm to our principles, reflecting light to the world. We should be alarmed at the least manifestation of a disposition to hush the voices that proclaim the third angel's message.** That angel represents the people of God, who give the last warning to the world. Let not the fear of man, the desire for patronage, be allowed to obscure a ray of heaven's light. Should the sentinels of truth now fail to sound the warning, they would be unworthy of their position as light-bearers to the world; but should the standard fall from their hands, the Lord would raise up others who would be faithful and loyal (*Review and Herald,* February 7, 1893).

The message we have to bear is not a message that men need to cringe to declare. They are not to seek to cover it, to conceal its origin and purpose. Its advocates must be men who will not hold their peace day nor night. As those who have made solemn vows to God, and who have been commissioned as the messengers of Christ, as stewards of the mysteries of the grace of God, **we are under obligation to declare faithfully the whole counsel of God. We are not to make less prominent the special truths that have separated us from the world and made us what we are; for they are fraught with eternal interests.** God has given us light in regard to the things that are now taking place in the last remnant of time, and with pen and voice we are to proclaim the truth to the world, not in a tame, spiritless way, but in demonstration of the Spirit and power of God. The mightiest conflicts are involved in the furtherance of the message, and the results of its promulgation are of moment to both heaven and earth (*Life Sketches of Ellen G. White,* p. 329).

Veiled spiritualism, as found in many popular churches, is not compatible with the unique Seventh-day Adventist message. **We are here on a special mission unlike that of any other church.**

In a special sense Seventh-day Adventists have been set in the world as watchmen and light-bearers. To them has been entrusted the last warning for a perishing world. On them is shining wonderful light from the Word of God. **They have been given a work of the most solemn import,—the proclamation of the first, second, and third angels' messages. There is no other work of so great importance. They are to allow nothing else to absorb their attention** (*Evangelism,* p. 119).

Revelation 14:6–12, NKJV

Then I saw another angel flying in the midst of heaven, having the everlasting gospel to preach to those who dwell on the earth—to every nation, tribe, tongue, and people—saying with a loud voice, "Fear God and give glory to Him, for the hour of His judgment has come; and worship Him who made heaven and earth, the sea and springs of water."

And another angel followed, saying, "Babylon is fallen, is fallen, that great city, because she has made all nations drink of the wine of the wrath of her fornication." Then a third angel followed them, saying with a loud voice, "If anyone worships the beast and his image, and receives his mark on his forehead or on his hand, he himself shall also drink of the wine of the wrath of God, which is poured out full strength into the cup of His indignation. And he shall be tormented with fire and brimstone in the presence of the holy angels and in the presence of the Lamb. And the smoke of their torment ascends forever and ever; and they have no rest day or night, who worship the beast and his image, and whoever receives the mark of his name." Here is the patience of the saints; here are those who keep the commandments of God and the faith of Jesus.

The three angels' messages are to be combined, giving their threefold light to the world. In the Revelation, John says, "I saw another angel come down from heaven, having great power; and the earth was lightened with his glory."

[Rev. 18:2-5 quoted]. **This represents the giving of the last and threefold message of warning to the world** (MS 52, 1900) (*Seventh-day Adventist Bible Commentary,* vol. 7, p. 985).

"We are as a people in danger of giving the third angel's message in such an indefinite manner that it does not impress the people. . . . **Our message is a life-and-death message, and we must let this message appear as it is, —the great power of God. Then the Lord will make it effectual. We are to present it in all its telling force** (*Evangelism,* p. 230).

In the cities of to-day, where there is so much to attract and please, the people can be interested by no ordinary efforts. Ministers of God's appointment will find it necessary to put forth extraordinary efforts in order to arrest the attention of multitudes. And when they succeed in bringing together a large number of people, they must bear messages of a character so out of the usual order that the people will be aroused and warned. **They must make use of every means that can possibly be devised for causing the truth to stand out clearly and distinctly.** The testing message for this time is to be borne so plainly and decidedly as to startle the hearers, and lead them to desire to study the Scriptures.

Those who do the work of the Lord in the cities must put forth calm, steady, devoted effort for the education of the people. While they are to labor earnestly to interest the hearers, and to hold this interest, yet at the same time they must carefully **guard against anything that borders on sensationalism.** In this age of extravagance and outward show, when men think it necessary to make a display in order to gain success, God's chosen messengers are to show the fallacy of spending means needlessly for effect. As they labor with simplicity, humility, and graceful dignity, **avoiding everything of a theatrical nature,** their work will make a lasting impression for good (*Gospel Workers,* pp. 345, 346).

Satan has devised a state of things whereby the proclamation of the third angel's message shall be bound about. **We must beware of his plans and methods. There must be no toning down of the truth, no muffling of the message for this time.** The third angel's message must be strengthened and confirmed. **The eighteenth chapter of Revelation reveals the importance of presenting the truth in no measured terms but with boldness and power. . . .** There has been too much beating about the bush in the proclamation of the third angel's message. The message has not been given as clearly and distinctly as it should have been (*Evangelism,* p. 230).

Do not make prominent those features of the message which are a condemnation of the customs and practices of the people, until they have opportunity to know that we are believers in Christ, that we believe in His divinity and in His pre-existence. Let the testimony of the world's Redeemer be dwelt upon (Ibid., p. 231).

The religionist generally has divorced the law and the gospel, while we have on the other hand almost done the same from another standpoint. We have not held up before the people the righteousness of Christ and the full significance of His great plan of redemption. We have left *out* Christ and His matchless love, and brought in the theories and reasonings, preached arguments (Ibid., pp. 231, 232).

If we would have the spirit and power of the third angel's message, we must present the law and the gospel together, for they go hand in hand (*Gospel Workers,* p. 161).

The followers of Christ are to combine in a strong effort to call the attention of the world to the fast-fulfilling prophecies of the Word of God (*Evangelism,* p. 193).

The days in which we live are times that call for constant vigilance, times in which God's people should be awake to do a great work in presenting the light on the Sabbath question. . . . This last warning to the inhabitants of the earth is to make men see the importance God attaches to His holy law. So plainly is the truth to be presented that no transgressor, hearing it, shall fail to discern the importance of obedience to the Sabbath commandment (Ibid., p. 232).

If ministers who are called upon to preach the most solemn message ever given to mortals, evade the truth, they are unfaithful in their work, and are false shepherds to the sheep and the lambs. The assertions of man are of no value. Let the Word of God speak to the people. Let those who have heard only traditions and maxims of men, hear the voice of God, whose promises are Yea and Amen in Christ Jesus. If the character and deportment of the shepherd is a living epistle to the people of the truth which he advocates, the Lord will set His seal to the work. True friendships will be formed with the people, and the shepherd and the flock will become one, united by a common hope in Christ Jesus (*Review and Herald,* March 11, 1902).

Would that every minister of God realized the holiness of his work and the sacredness of his office. As divinely appointed messengers, ministers are in a position of awful responsibility. **They are to reprove, rebuke, exhort, with all long-suffering. In Christ's stead they are to labor as stewards of the mysteries of heaven, encouraging the obedient, and warning the disobedient.** Worldly policy is to have no weight with them. Never are they to swerve from the plain path in which Jesus has bidden them walk. They are to go forward in faith, remembering that they are surrounded by a cloud of witnesses. **They are not to speak their own words, but the words which One greater than the potentates of earth has bidden them speak. Their message is to be, "Thus saith the Lord." God**

calls for men like Elijah, Nathan, and John the Baptist, men who will bear His message with faithfulness, regardless of the consequences, who will speak the truth bravely, though it calls for the sacrifice of all they have (Ibid., October 22, 1901).

Revelation 18:1–5, NKJV

After these things I saw another angel coming down from heaven, having great authority, and the earth was illuminated with his glory. And he cried mightily with a loud voice, saying, "Babylon the great is fallen, is fallen, and has become a dwelling place of demons, a prison for every foul spirit, and a cage for every unclean and hated bird! For all the nations have drunk of the wine of the wrath of her fornication, the kings of the earth have committed fornication with her, and the merchants of the earth have become rich through the abundance of her luxury." And I heard another voice from heaven saying, "Come out of her, my people, lest you share in her sins, and lest you receive of her plagues. For her sins have reached to heaven, and God has remembered her iniquities."

God has given the messages of Revelation 14 their place in the line of prophecy and their work is not to cease till the close of this earth's history.

Revelation 18 points to the time when, as the result of rejecting the threefold warning of Revelation 14:6-12, the church will have fully reached the condition foretold by the second angel, and the people of God still in Babylon will be called upon to separate from her communion. This message is the last that will ever be given to the world (*Last Day Events,* pp. 198, 199).

This scripture points forward to a time when the announcement of the fall of Babylon, as made by the second angel of Revelation 14 (verse 8), is to be repeated, with the additional mention of the corruptions which have been entering the various organizations that constitute Babylon, since that message was first given, in the summer of 1844. A terrible condition of the religious world is here described. With every rejection of truth the minds of the people will become darker, their hearts more stubborn, until they are entrenched in an infidel hardihood. In defiance of the warnings which God has given, **they will continue to trample upon one of the precepts of the Decalogue,** until they are led to persecute those who hold it sacred. Christ is set at nought in the contempt placed upon His word and His people. **As the teachings of spiritualism are accepted by the churches,** the restraint imposed upon the carnal heart is removed, and the profession of religion will become a cloak to conceal the basest iniquity. A belief in spiritual manifestations opens the door to seducing spirits, and doctrines of devils, and thus the influence of evil angels will be felt in the churches (*The Great Controversy,* pp. 603, 604).

[Rev. 18:1-3, quoted.] While this message is sounding, while the proclamation of truth is doing its separat-

SPIRITUALISM IN MODERN DRESS

ing work, we as faithful sentinels of God are to discern what our real position is. We are not to confederate with worldlings, lest we become imbued with their spirit, lest our spiritual discernment become confused and we view those who have the truth and bear the message of the Lord from the standpoint of the professed Christian churches. At the same time we are not to be like the Pharisees and hold ourselves aloof from them (*Last Day Events,* pp. 84, 85).

God's message will end with power and strength

Although truth has never been popular, and certainly is not popular now, it will end with power and strength. The honest in heart will respond to God's call before Jesus returns. The whole earth will be lightened with the influence of heaven.

The truth of God has never been popular with the world. The natural heart is ever averse to the truth. I thank God that we must renounce the love of the world, and pride of heart, and everything which tends to idolatry, in order to be followers of the Man of Calvary. **Those who obey the truth will never be loved and honored by the world** (*Testimonies for the Church,* vol. 2, p. 491).

In visions of the night, representations passed before me of **a great reformatory movement among God's people. Many were praising God. The sick were healed, and other miracles were wrought.** A spirit of intercession was seen, even as was manifested before the great Day

97

of Pentecost. Hundreds and thousands were seen visiting families and opening before them the word of God. Hearts were convicted by the power of the Holy Spirit, and a spirit of genuine conversion was manifest. On every side doors were thrown open to the proclamation of the truth. The world seemed to be lightened with the heavenly influence. Great blessings were received by the true and humble people of God. I heard voices of thanksgiving and praise, and there seemed to be a reformation such as we witnessed in 1844.

Yet some refused to be converted. They were not willing to walk in God's way, and when, in order that the work of God might be advanced, calls were made for free-will offerings, some clung selfishly to their earthly possessions. These covetous ones became separated from the company of believers (Ibid., vol. 9, p. 126).

Why has the history of the work of the disciples, as they labored with holy zeal, animated and vitalized by the Holy Spirit, been recorded, if it is not that from this record the Lord's people today are to gain an inspiration to work earnestly for Him? What the Lord did for His people in that time, it is just as essential, and more so, that He do for His people today. **All that the apostles did, every church member today is to do.** And we are to work with as much more fervor, to be accompanied by the Holy Spirit in as much greater measure, as the increase of wickedness demands a more decided call to repentance (Ibid., vol. 7, p. 33).

I saw that this message will close with power and strength far exceeding the midnight cry.

Servants of God, endowed with power from on high, with their faces lighted up, and shining with holy consecration, went forth to proclaim the message from heaven. Souls that were scattered all through the religious bodies answered to the call, and the precious were hurried out of the doomed churches, as Lot was hurried out of Sodom before her destruction. God's people were strengthened by the excellent glory which rested upon them in rich abundance, and prepared them to endure the hour of temptation. I heard everywhere a multitude of voices saying, "Here is the patience of the saints; here are they that keep the commandments of God, and the faith of Jesus" (*Early Writings,* pp. 278, 279).

Those who have held the beginning of their confidence firm unto the end will be wide-awake during the time that the third angel's message is proclaimed with great power. During the loud cry, the church, aided by the providential interpositions of her exalted Lord, will diffuse the knowledge of salvation so abundantly that light will be communicated to every city and town. The earth will be filled with the knowledge of salvation. So abundantly will the renewing Spirit of God have crowned with success the intensely active agencies, that the light of present truth will be seen flashing everywhere (*Maranatha,* p. 218).

CHAPTER
7

SATAN'S PLANS FOR THE REMNANT CHURCH

1. Bring in the extreme of either cold formalism or fanaticism.

He [Satan] is working with all his insinuating, deceiving power, to lead men away from the third angel's message, which is to be proclaimed with mighty power. If Satan sees that the Lord is blessing His people and preparing them to discern his delusions, **he will work with his master power to bring in fanaticism on the one hand and cold formalism on the other**, that he may gather in a harvest of souls. Now is our time to watch unceasingly. Watch, bar the way to the least step of advance that Satan may make among you (*Selected Messages*, bk. 1, pp. 19, 20).

I was shown the churches in different states that profess to be keeping the commandments of God and looking for the second coming of Christ. There is an alarming amount of **indifference, pride, love of the world, and cold formality** existing among them. And these are the people who are fast coming to resemble ancient Israel, so far as the want of piety is concerned. **Many make high claims to godliness and yet are destitute of self-control.** Appetite and passion bear sway; self is made prominent. **Many are arbitrary, dictatorial, overbearing, boastful, proud, and unconsecrated.** Yet some of these persons are ministers, handling sacred truths. Unless they repent, their candlestick will be removed out of its place. The Saviour's curse pronounced upon the fruitless fig tree is a sermon to all formalists and boasting hypocrites who stand forth to the world in pretentious leaves, but are devoid of fruit. What a rebuke to those who have a form of godliness, while in their unchristian lives they deny the power thereof! He who treated with tenderness the very chief of sinners, He who never spurned true meekness and penitence, however great the guilt, came down with scathing denunciations upon those who made high professions of godliness, but in works denied their faith (*Testimonies for the Church,* vol. 4, pp. 403, 404).

2. Keep members in lethargy and stupor while they live in sin.

Never was there greater need of faithful warnings and reproofs, and close, straight dealing, than at this very time. Satan has come down with great power, knowing that his time is short. He is flooding the world with pleasing fables, and **the people of God love to have smooth things spoken to them. Sin and iniquity are not abhorred.** I was shown that God's people must make more firm, determined efforts to press back the incoming darkness. The close work of the Spirit of God is needed now as never before. Stupidity must be shaken off. We must arouse from the lethargy that will prove our destruction unless we resist it. Satan has a powerful, controlling influence upon minds. **Preachers and people are in danger of being found upon the side of the powers of darkness.** There is no such thing now as a neutral position. We are all decidedly for the right or decidedly with the wrong. Said Christ, "He that is not with Me is against Me; and he that gathereth not with Me scattereth abroad." (*Testimonies for the Church,* vol. 3, pp. 327, 328).

3. Lead members to be content with the form of godliness without the power.

As the people of God approach the perils of the last days, Satan holds earnest consultation with his angels as to the most successful plans of overthrowing their faith. He sees that the popular churches are lulled to sleep by his deceptive power. By pleasing sophistry and lying wonders he can continue to hold them under his control. Therefore he directs his angels to lay their snares especially for those who are looking for the second advent of Christ, and endeavoring to keep all the commandments of Jesus.

Says the deceiver: "We must exert all our wisdom and subtlety to deceive and ensnare those who honor the true Sabbath. We can separate many from Christ by worldliness, lust, and pride. They may think themselves safe because they believe the truth, but indulgence of appetite and the lower passions, which confuse judgment and destroy discrimination, will cause them to fall.

"Through those who have a form of godliness, but know not the power, we may gain many. Those who are lovers of pleasure more than lovers of God will be our most effective helpers. **Those of this class who are apt and intelligent will draw others into their snares. Many will not fear their influence, because they profess the same faith. We will lead them to conclude that the requirements of God are less strict than they once believed, and that by conforming to the world they will exert a greater influence with worldlings. Thus they will separate from Christ. Then they will have no strength to resist our power; and ere long they will be ready to ridicule their former zeal and devotion**" (*Australasian Union Conference Record*, April 15, 1912).

4. Stir up members to criticize, judge, and condemn one another.

[Satan to his angels:] "We must cause distraction and division. We must destroy their anxiety for their own souls, and lead them to criticize, to judge and accuse and condemn one another, and to cherish selfishness and enmity. For these sins God banished us from His presence, and all who follow our example will meet a similar fate.

"Go, make the possessors of lands and money drunk

with the cares of this life. Present the world before them in its most attractive light that they may lay up their treasure here, and fix their affections on earthly things. We must do our utmost to prevent those who labor in God's cause from obtaining means to use against us. Keep the money in our own ranks. The more means they obtain, the more they will injure our kingdom by taking from us our subjects. Make them care more for money than for the building up of Christ's kingdom and the spread of the truths we hate, and we need not fear their influence; for we know that every selfish, covetous person will fall under our power, and will be separated finally from God's people."

So subtle and untiring are the efforts of the enemy of souls, that God's people need to be very watchful, and to labor earnestly and unceasingly to counterwork evil in the church and in the world. Satan and his agencies are laying out special lines of labor for those who are controlled by his power. Deceptions of every kind and degree are arising, so that if possible he would deceive the very elect. With the same subtle power that he plotted for the rebellion of holy beings in heaven before the fall, Satan is working today to operate through human beings for the fulfillment of his purposes of evil (*Australasian Union Conference Record*, April 15, 1912).

These are just a few of the ways Satan will work against the church. You will find many more as you study this subject further.

CHAPTER
8

A FINAL WORD
OF CAUTION

Veiled spiritualism has prepared the way for Satan to work in many Sunday-keeping churches because he has skillfully kept hidden the law of God. Some Adventist churches could be infected unconsciously by studying and following their ideas—reading only what seems acceptable, overlooking what is obviously unacceptable, and not recognizing what is **not** said. What we need to realize is that the mission and message of these megachurches are wrapped up together.

In light of the subtle form in which spiritualism will gain entrance to mainline churches, let's review again the look of this clever evil. Spiritualism is not just séances in a darkened room, the appearance of the dead who speak to us, or even variations of New Age teachings. Veiled spiritualism dresses in the clothes of mainline Christianity. Yet the end result leads one away from Jesus even while he or she professes to love and serve Jesus. At the same time, it opens the door for direct communication from the evil spirits. It happens like this:

- The Bible is interpreted in a manner that is pleasing to

the unrenewed heart, while its solemn and vital truths are made of no effect.

- Love is dwelt upon as the chief attribute of God, but it is degraded to a weak sentimentalism, making little distinction between good and evil.

- God's justice, His denunciations of sin, the requirements of His holy law, are all kept out of sight. The people are taught to regard the Decalogue as virtually Ten Suggestions.

- For some of these churches, pleasing, bewitching fables and skits captivate the senses and lead individuals to minimize the Bible as the foundation of their faith.

- The Christ who opened His ministry by proclaiming "Repent and believe" is obscured by emphasizing only His forgiveness, by confusing confession with repentance. But the eyes of the people are blinded so they don't see the deception.

With this worldview accepted by the majority of Christians, it will be easy for Satan to come in the form of departed loved ones—or, at the end, as Jesus Himself. These deceptions will lead many in a final rejection of God and His law. They have believed a lie, thus there is no protection from the final deception. Even Adventists who have this viewpoint will go along with those who have, step by step, compromised their thinking and who have chosen to disobey the law of God.

A FINAL WORD OF CAUTION

Satan is striving to gain every advantage. . . . **Disguised as an angel of light, he will walk the earth as a wonder-worker. In beautiful language he will present lofty sentiments; good words will be spoken by him and good deeds performed. Christ will be personified. But on one point there will be a marked distinction—Satan will turn the people from the law of God.** Notwithstanding this, so well will he counterfeit righteousness that, if it were possible, he would deceive the very elect. Crowned heads, presidents, rulers in high places, will bow to his false theories (*Last Day Events,* p. 166).

The time is not far distant when the test will come to every soul. The mark of the beast will be urged upon us. **Those who have step by step yielded to worldly demands and conformed to worldly customs will not find it a hard matter to yield to the powers that be, rather than subject themselves to derision, insult, threatened imprisonment, and death. The contest is between the commandments of God and the commandments of men.** In this time the gold will be separated from the dross in the church (Ibid., pp. 173, 174).

As the storm approaches, a large class who have professed faith in the third angel's message, but **have not been sanctified through obedience to the truth,** abandon their position and join the ranks of the opposition (*The Great Controversy,* p. 608).

In Paul's second epistle to the Thessalonians, he exhorts to be on guard, and not depart from the faith. **He speaks of Christ's coming as an event to immediately follow the work of Satan in spiritualism** in these words: "Even him, whose coming is after the working of Satan with all power and signs and lying wonders, and with all deceivableness of unrighteousness in them that perish; because they received not the love of the truth, that they might be saved. And for this cause God shall send them strong delusion, that they should believe a lie; that they all might be damned who **believed not the truth, but had pleasure in unrighteousness**" (*Signs of the Times,* April 12, 1883).

Satan has long been preparing for his final effort to deceive the world. The foundation of his work was laid by the assurance given to Eve in Eden: "Ye shall not surely die." "In the day ye eat thereof, then your eyes shall be opened, and ye shall be as gods, knowing good and evil." Genesis 3:4, 5. **Little by little he has prepared the way for his masterpiece of deception in the development of spiritualism.** He has not yet reached the full accomplishment of his designs; but it will be reached in the last remnant of time. Says the prophet: "I saw three unclean spirits like frogs; . . . they are the spirits of devils, working miracles, which go forth unto the kings of the earth and of the whole world, to gather them to the battle of that great day of God Almighty." Revelation 16:13, 14. **Except those who are kept by the power of God,**

through faith in His word, the whole world will be swept into the ranks of this delusion. The people are fast being lulled to a fatal security, to be awakened only by the outpouring of the wrath of God (*The Great Controversy,* pp. 561, 562).

We need not be deceived. Wonderful scenes, with which Satan will be closely connected, will soon take place. God's Word declares that Satan will work miracles. He will make people sick, and then will suddenly remove from them his satanic power. They will then be regarded as healed. These works of apparent healing will bring Seventh-day Adventists to the test. Many who have had great light will fail to walk in the light, because they have not become one with Christ (*Selected Messages,* book 2, p. 53).

Our positive approach
Adventists find their strength in remembering why we exist. We were raised up for one purpose: to prepare a people for translation. We are in the end of the end time. Some generation will surely be the last! We have the awesome challenge of preparing the honest seekers of truth for God's seal of approval described in Revelation 7 and 14. Peter's appeal (2 Peter 3:10–14) will describe that last-day group for which God waits. Our privilege is to join this group and to invite all others from every Christian denomination, from every religious body in the world, to hear our gracious Lord's call, "Come!"

We can be victorious

If all we have been describing and that is soon to come upon this planet seems a bit overwhelming, maybe even discouraging, remember that you have a Friend in Jesus who is more than able to bring you through victorious.

Satan assailed Christ with his fiercest and most subtle temptations; but he was repulsed in every conflict. Those battles were fought in our behalf; those victories make it possible for us to conquer. **Christ will give strength to all who seek it. No man without his own consent can be overcome by Satan.** The tempter has no power to control the will or to force the soul to sin. He may distress, but he cannot contaminate. He can cause agony, but not defilement. The fact that Christ has conquered should inspire his followers with courage to fight manfully the battle against sin and Satan (*The Great Controversy,* p. 510).

How to share what you know

This study has been compiled for the use of Adventist church leaders, pastors, and members to better acquaint them with contemporary issues in the great controversy. Some will be tempted to use it as a hammer against those who are committed to doing things differently so they can grow the church. Or there may be a church near you on a dangerous course as outlined in this book. Some may not agree with the conclusions or concerns of this study. Whatever the case may be, it would be wise to keep in mind the following counsel as we engage in conversation with others:

A FINAL WORD OF CAUTION

If Christ is in you "the hope of glory," you will have no disposition to watch others, to expose their errors. Instead of seeking to accuse and condemn, it will be your object to help, to bless, and to save. In dealing with those who are in error, you will heed the injunction, Consider "thyself, lest thou also be tempted." Galatians 6:1. You will call to mind the many times you have erred and how hard it was to find the right way when you had once left it. You will not push your brother into greater darkness, but with a heart full of pity will tell him of his danger.

He who looks often upon the cross of Calvary, remembering that his sins placed the Saviour there, will never try to estimate the degree of his guilt in comparison with that of others. He will not climb upon the judgment seat to bring accusation against another. There can be no spirit of criticism or self-exaltation on the part of those who walk in the shadow of Calvary's cross.

Not until you feel that you could sacrifice your own self-dignity, and even lay down your life in order to save an erring brother, have you cast the beam out of your own eye so that you are prepared to help your brother. Then you can approach him and touch his heart. No one has ever been reclaimed from a wrong position by censure and reproach; but many have thus been driven from Christ and led to seal their hearts against conviction. A tender spirit, a gentle, winning deportment, may save the erring and hide a multitude of sins. The revelation of Christ in your own character will have a transforming power upon all with whom you come in contact. Let Christ be daily made manifest in you, and He will reveal through you the creative energy of His word—a gentle, persuasive, yet mighty influence to re-create other souls in the beauty of the Lord our God (*Thoughts From the Mount of Blessing*, pp. 128, 129).

Brethren, if a man is overtaken in any trespass, you who are spiritual restore such a one in a spirit of gentleness, considering yourself lest you also be tempted. Bear one another's burdens, and so fulfill the law of Christ. For if anyone thinks himself to be something, when he is nothing, he deceives himself (Galatians 6:1–3, NKJV).